The Big Book of Jokes

The Big Book

of Jokes

selected and told by HELEN HOKE
pictures by RICHARD ERDOES

FRANKLIN WATTS | NEW YORK | LONDON

BOOK DESIGN BY J.M. KUPFER

Contents

About This Book

Right after I'd finished my first book of jokes, JOKES, JOKES, JOKES, I swore I'd never do another! I swore it to my publisher. My husband. My son. His children. And all my friends.

It was too much, I said. Riddles and rhymes were going around in my head like voodoo drumbeats, my dreams were full of clowns with large wobbling noses and hideous tearstained faces, and when friends started off an evening with "Have you heard the one about—?" I made un-friends of some of them by hastily muttering, "Yes, yes!" before they could tell me. So, you may well ask, Why *have* you written another? (Well, actually, I've written *two* others.)

You see, people just wouldn't stop telling me jokes. Or sending me cartoons. Or asking me riddles. Or filing away jokes torn from magazines and letters and newspapers and marking them, "Remember to send to H.H." So, after a while, jokes began to seem funny again. Then, several years ago, I had occasion to go around the world on a speaking tour.

I went first to Bangkok, Hong Kong, Sydney, New Zealand, then on to the Fiji Islands, then to Los Angeles, Chicago, New York, and back to London again. In New Zealand I visited a hospital for children. Some of the children were very ill, some were crippled, some were recovering from accidents. But, you know, they were nearly all *smiling*. That crusty old feeling that I'd tucked away inside me labeled "Sense of humor—no longer working" received a funny kind of uplift: if *these* children could laugh and tell jokes and smile up at the sun, why couldn't *I*?

So I started all over again. Listening. Reading. Trading stories with friends who knew a great many. Paying twenty-five cents for each joke I had not heard before, to some boys and girls who had always been my dependable helpers. My study became packed with index cards and filing boxes and scraps of paper; my husband began putting clippings from newspapers on my desk again and even my grandchildren started to torment me once more with riddles like "What's soft and yellow and goes round and round?" (A long-playing omelet, of course.)

My second book was called MORE JOKES, JOKES, JOKES and young people seemed to like it, and asked for more.

So, now, here's my third—a bumper book of jokes that has taken three years to compile. But—you know something?—it's been fun!

Happy joke-swapping!

Helen Hoke

LONDON
SPRING, 1971

The Big Book of Jokes

Animal Antics

The new farmhand asked the farmer how long cows should be milked.

"The same as the short ones," the farmer replied laconically.

Dumb Dora reports that her boyfriend promised her a mink for her birthday . . . . but on one condition. She asked what it was, prepared to refuse indignantly.

"That you keep its cage clean," he replied.

Curious Carl, staring out of the window one day, noticed a commotion going on in the litter basket on the street corner. He raced out to investigate and came back completely satisfied that the right thing had been done: behind the sign PLACE LITTER HERE he had discovered a spaniel and her five pups.

•

The traveling salesman's horse dropped dead suddenly on Punxsutawney Street—in a small Pennsylvania town. The policeman on the beat strolled up, pulled out his book, and prepared to make out his report. Then he paused and glanced about the crowd that had gathered.

"How do you spell Punxsutawney?" he asked.

There was a general shaking of heads.

"Okay," he sighed, closing up his book. "A few of you fellows give me a hand and we'll haul this animal into Main Street."

•

A mother hen was anxious to hear what her two little chickens had learned in school that day. The first one said, "peep peep." She was delighted that he was learning to speak so well.

Then she turned to his brother and asked what *he* had learned. "Cuckoo," he replied. When she looked puzzled he explained, "I'm taking a foreign language this semester."

•

Small boy to friend, watching TV: "same old story . . . boy gets dog, boy loses dog, boy finds dog."

The little rabbit kept pestering its mother with questions about where it had come from.

Finally she turned on him impatiently. "All right, if you *must* know, you were pulled out of a magician's top hat on the stage of the Palace Theater at a Friday night performance. *Now* will you stop bothering me?"

The baggage car of a very slow Southern train contained five sacks of mail, a battered trunk, nine packages—and one live mule with a destination tag tied around his neck.

Just before the train reached Athens, the mule chewed up the tag. Mose, the brakeman, discovered the loss and exclaimed, "Now what is we gonna do wid dis crazy mule? He done et up where he's goin'."

A bored cat and an interested cat were watching a tennis match.

"You seem very interested in tennis," said the bored cat.

"It's not that," said the interested cat, "but my old man's in the racket."

What did the pony say when it coughed?
Excuse me, I'm a little hoarse.

A new species appeared in the local pet shop. Curious Carl immediately went to investigate and came home to report to his sister.

SISTER: What is it, Carl?

CARL: A cross between a parrot and a tiger.

SISTER: Does it talk?

CARL: Only a little. But when it *does* say something . . . run!

•

A showman was trying to sell a new act to a traveling circus. The manager agreed to give him a few minutes and followed the man to his car. From the trunk, he took out a small poodle, a Siamese cat, and a clarinet.

The cat began to play the clarinet and the poodle sang out in a strong tenor a very creditable version of "The Star-Spangled Banner."

"You're hired!" cried the manager. "That's a wonderful act."

The showman struggled with his conscience for a few minutes, and then he decided to confess.

"I've been deceiving you, sir," he said. "The poodle can't really sing at all. The cat is a ventriloquist."

An imaginative park commissioner suggested it would be a nice idea to have a gondola on the lake in Central Park.

"Marvelous!" exclaimed his secretary. "But why not order two—a male and a female?"

Thoughtful Thelma worried and worried as she and a companion drove through the autumn countryside. Finally she turned and said, "You know that sign we keep passing that says Warning, Deer Crossing?"

"Sure," said the driver of the car. "I always look out for them."

"I know," she said, "but how do the deer *know* that's where they're supposed to cross?"

•

ADDLEPATED AL: Why does an elephant have a trunk?
EDUCATED EDDIE: Because it doesn't have a glove compartment, silly!

The young philosopher, who liked to prove that old adages are right, packed up his violin and went into the jungle . . . to demonstrate that "music has charms to soothe a savage beast."

He found a watering hole and began to play. Within minutes there had gathered around him an elephant, a tiger, three monkeys, and a boa constrictor. Motionless they listened to the strains of a sonata.

Then, just before the end of the first movement, without a word of warning, the tiger sprang and killed the philosopher with one mighty blow. The others turned on the tiger and berated him for spoiling their concert.

"How could you do a thing like that?" trumpeted the elephant.

"If you had a decent ear instead of a useless trunk," snarled the tiger, "you'd know that he played an A for an A-sharp."

•

A nearsighted hunter took aim at a large body moving among the trees and saw it drop.

"What," he exclaimed in great excitement to his companion, "have I brought down with such a perfect shot?"

"I'm not sure, old buddy," said his friend, "but between curses it's saying that its name is MacIntosh!"

•

The new farmhand, wanting to show how clever he was, said to his employer, "Do you know how to get the hens to lay boiled eggs?"

"Are you daft?" asked the farmer.

"Why not at all, sir. Just feed them boiling water!"

One morning, a tenderhearted bachelor, out for a stroll, passed a restaurant, where he noticed a mangy little kitten lapping up milk from a saucer. The saucer, he realized with a start, was an extremely valuable and rare piece of pottery.

He walked casually into the store and offered three dollars for the cat. "It's not for sale," said the proprietor. "Look," said the man, who was a collector of objets d'art, "that cat is dirty and undesirable, but I'm eccentric. I *like* cats that way. I'll raise my offer to five dollars."

"It's a deal," said the proprietor, putting the five-dollar bill into his pocket.

"For the extra money I'm sure you won't mind throwing in the saucer," said the collector. "The kitten seems so happy drinking from it."

"Nothing doing," said the proprietor firmly. "That saucer belonged to my beloved grandmother. Also, from that saucer, so far this week, I've sold thirty-four cats."

•

SILLY SALLY: Every day my dog and I go for a tramp in the woods.
SILLY SAM: You and your dog must enjoy that.
SILLY SALLY: We love it, but the tramp's getting awfully cranky about it.

•

Timid Tilly was supposed to have been asleep hours ago, but she kept calling downstairs that there was a spider on the ceiling of her bedroom.

"Oh, Tilly," her father called up to her in disgust. "You're certainly not afraid of a little spider, are you?"

"Then why am I hiding in the bathroom?" she sobbed.

A shaggy dog was crossing a stream with a piece of meat in its mouth. Looking down, it saw its own reflection in the water and, thinking that it was another dog carrying a better piece of meat, dropped its own hunk and dove down to snatch at the better-looking piece of meat.

Of course there was no other dog at the bottom of the stream, but in the meantime a large trout swam by and seized the meat. The dog's jaws clamped over the trout; then it swam to the bank of the stream and trotted off cheerfully.

You see, the dog preferred freshly caught fish to meat.

•

A merchant from upstate New York drove his horse and his wagon loaded with produce to a neighboring market.

On the way, he met a farmer he knew, who asked him, "What are you selling today?"

The farmer leaned over and whispered in his ear, "Oats."

"Why the secrecy?" demanded the other farmer.

"S-s-sh," said the first farmer, "not so loud. I don't want my horse to hear."

•

FIRST GUINEA PIG: You know, I've finally got that scientist conditioned.

SECOND GUINEA PIG: Oh, what makes you think so?

FIRST GUINEA PIG: Every time I go through that maze and ring the bell, he gives me something to eat!

•

GOOFY GUS: Did you know that insects can cry?

CLEVER CLARA: Sure. Haven't you ever seen a mothball?

Business Boners

A big business tycoon called a dozen of his creditors together to tell them that he was about to go into bankruptcy. "I owe you over twenty thousand dollars," he said in a matter-of-fact voice, "and my assets aren't enough to pay you a nickel on the dollar. So," he went on, teetering back and forth on his heels, "I rather imagine it will be impossible for you to get anything—unless"—he smiled— "you want to cut me up in parts and divide me among you."

"Mr. Chairman," said one of the creditors, "I move we do this. And *I'd* like to have his gall."

Clever Chris has some fairly untechnical definitions about a few things. A sample: The difference between gross and net income is . . . plenty!

"Show me! Just *show* me," the irritated boss roared, "one single order that advertising ever put on our books!"

"I will do just that," retorted his advertising manager, "the first time you show *me* a single load of hay that the sun ever put into a barn!"

•

A very, very rich man, being interviewed about his self-made fortune, confided, "I never hesitate to give full credit to my wife for her assistance."

"Oh, is that so: in what way did *she* help?" the reporter asked.

"Well, if you want the whole truth," replied the wealthy man, "I was curious to find out if there was any income she couldn't live beyond."

•

A letter to a mail-order house:
Sir:
Would you please send me the vacuum cleaner you advertise on page 181 of your current catalog? If it's any good, I'll send you a check.

The reply:
Madam:
Please send us your check. If it's any good, we'll send you the vacuum cleaner.

•

ANGRY BOSS: If you cannot manage your work better than this, I shall be forced to get another clerk!
LAZY CLERK: Oh, thank you, sir—I could use some help!

The beautiful redhead graduated (with few honors) from secretarial school and applied for her first job. It was with a shipbuilding firm.

"Can you read a blueprint?" the personnel manager asked her.

"Oh yes," she replied confidently. "I can read any color print at all!"

•

Once, after his retirement, the great financier Andrew Carnegie was asked which facet of industry he considered most important—capital, labor, or brains.

"Well," he replied, "I think I'll let you answer that question yourself: which is the most important leg of a three-legged stool?"

•

A man who handles the complaint desk at a large Chicago public service organization has worked out a devastatingly efficient technique for squelching unreasonable beefers. After a telephone caller has spent some time working up into a bitter tirade against the organization, complete with many details and examples, the complaint man waits till the angry caller reaches the sputtering point, then breaks in with, "Pardon me, madam, I was called away from the phone. . . . Would you mind repeating what you just said?"

•

Cheerful wife, to homecoming husband: "Did you win tonight, darling?"

"Don't be silly, dear, I was playing the boss!"

Capital Capers

Abraham Lincoln was superbly equipped to deal with hecklers. After one of his speeches a farmer stood up and said, "Say, Mr. Lincoln, that speech of yours was pretty fair—but there was some points you brung up that was beyond my reach."

Lincoln chuckled as he replied, "Well, sir, I'm right sorry for you. I once had a dog that had the very same trouble with fleas!"

In a recent election, a voter was undecided which candidate he favored for congressman from his district. He decided to make a test. He knocked on candidate A's door one night and said, "I need a little help. My car went dead. How about giving me a push?"

"I'll do better than that, my friend," said the candidate. "I'll call the garage for you. Just wait in your car. I'm sure they'll be around soon."

The voter then started up his engine and headed for Candidate B's house, repeating his plea for assistance.

"Sure," was the answer this time. The would-be congressman rolled up his sleeves and headed for the car. The owner walked ahead of him, got in the car and started up his engine. Grinning broadly, he said, "You have *my* vote, mister. I like to know that the man who's down in Washington representing me takes things into his own hands!"

•

During the depression, in the thirties, experts were called to Washington by the hundreds to find the solution to the nation's difficulties. To put it simply: where to find some money.

One evening President Roosevelt planned a little entertainment to lighten the life of his staff, and just before the announced time for dinner a famous magician drove up to the door of the White House.

"Who are you?" asked the guard, "and what are your credentials?"

The magician simply reached out and produced a shiny new silver dollar from the air.

The guard heaved a great sigh of relief and exclaimed, "At last!"

President Calvin Coolidge, nicknamed, for good reason, Silent Cal, had a reserve that sometimes went beyond belief—and sometimes proved embarrassing to those about him.

When Queen Marie of Romania visited the White House, he didn't address a single word to his distinguished guest until she was saying her thank-yous and preparing to depart. Then, as if to make up for his neglect, he said abuptly:

"Queen, what country are you from?"

•

Wise Wilfred says that the candidate's promises of today are the taxes of tomorrow.

When a distinguished lawyer in a western state was approached and asked if he would be his party's nominee for U.S. senator, he said, "I'd better phone my wife and see how she feels about it."

He called and said, "How would you like to be the wife of a United States senator?"

She thought about it for a moment and then asked, "Which one?"

•

Just after his election to the presidency in 1912, Woodrow Wilson visited an ancient and august aunt who was almost deaf. She asked him what he was doing now, and he shouted into her ear trumpet (rather proudly) that he was now the President of the United States.

"Of what?" inquired the old lady.

"Of the U.S.A.," Wilson shouted back.

His aunt closed the discussion by snorting, "Don't be silly!"

•

There have always been hecklers, and there will always be hecklers. Benjamin Franklin had a way of dealing with one of them:

He used to speak often about the Constitution of the United States, explaining the then new document. One day a heckler stood up and bawled, "Aw, them words don't mean nothing at all! Where's all that happiness you say it guarantees us?"

Old Ben smiled blandly and replied, "My friend, the Constitution guarantees you only the right to *pursue* happiness. You have to catch up with it *yourself*!"

Once President Theodore Roosevelt wanted for private reasons to travel incognito by train. He found himself stalled for several hours at a remote hamlet in Arkansas and, becoming impatient, revealed his identity to the porter and asked if something couldn't be done to get the train moving again.

"Look," said the porter, "even if you were the stationmaster's son, it wouldn't make any difference."

Many people we run across have no first or middle names, only initials. This was the case with D. G. Halpin. When he went to work for the government he carefully filled out all the forms (in triplicate, naturally) as D (only) G (only) Halpin. Sure enough, when D. G. got his first paycheck, it was made out to Donly Gonly Halpin.

•

One of the great presidents of the United States was one of the first people invited to try out a new invention . . . the telephone. He picked it up, said a few words into it, and received a clear reply from the other end.

"Well now," he said, putting it down, "it's a very remarkable thing, but who in blazes would ever want to *use* one of those contraptions?"

•

President Truman greeted a newly elected congressman during his first few days in the White House, and said in a kindly way, "I know just how you must feel. For the first six months you wonder how the devil you got here, and for the second six months you wonder how the devil the rest of 'em got here!"

Dizzy Domesticity

The newlyweds were living on a very tight budget, and the young bride had figured out every possible different way to serve a hamburger. On the fourteenth day her husband sat down to dinner, looked wearily at the new version, and murmured, "How now, ground chow?"

•

An absentminded scientist suddenly decided one day that he was being neglectful of his family. So that evening he went home, kissed his wife and children, shaved, showered, and changed before dinner, and exerted himself to tell several amusing stories during the meal.

When it was over he whistled as he cleared the table and insisted on washing and drying all the dishes by himself.

When he had tidied everything up he went into the living room to find his wife in tears.

"Everything's gone wrong today," she sobbed. "The Hoover broke down, Georgie threw a baseball through our bedroom window, Polly fell and tore her best dress—and now you come home so drunk you don't know what you're doing!"

•

Mr. Bigfamily complains *his* problem is "having too much month left over at the end of my money!"

A very pretty, demure-seeming young bride was on trial for shooting her aged, ill-tempered husband. The jury knew she was guilty, but not one of them wanted to convict her.

After deliberating for some hours they returned to the courtroom and asked whether her husband had belonged to any clubs or organizations.

"Yes," she said, "the Elks Club."

The jury retired to the jury room and in five minutes returned with the verdict: "Twenty-five dollars fine for shooting an Elk out of season."

A ballplayer, left in charge of a baby cousin, suddenly realized that he did not have the least idea how to change a diaper. Frantically, he called a friend who was, luckily, a father. The friend calmed down the ballplayer, then gave him the following instructions:

"Place the diaper in the position of a baseball diamond, with you at bat. Fold second base over home plate. Place baby on pitcher's mound, then pin first base and third base at home plate!"

HORACE: Did they take an X-ray photo of your wife's jaw at the hospital?

MORRIS: They tried to, but all they could get was a moving picture.

•

MISSUS: Would you like turkey for dinner tonight, darling?

MISTER: What's the alternative?

MISSUS: No dinner.

•

The lawyer listened patiently but uneasily while his client tearfully related the long-drawn-out story of her unhappy life with her husband. When she paused to wipe away her tears, he inquired:

"Just what do you want me to do?"

"Sue him for breach of promise!" the woman cried.

"But you've been married to him for thirteen years!" the startled lawyer protested.

"I know!" agreed the unhappy wife. "But seven years ago he promised me a divorce!"

•

MISTER: Darling, I brought some things home for the one I love best. I bet you can't guess what they are.

MISSUS: Razor blades, cigars, and a power drill.

•

A prospector's wife asked him to name the new mine after her. He agreed.

Ever since, one of the richest gold mines in the Black Hills of South Dakota has been known as The Holy Terror.

A man said on his silver wedding anniversary that the secret of his happy marriage was that every Valentine's Day he got down on his knees and proposed to his wife all over again.

"The only thing is that *now* when I get down," he added, "I don't just say
'I love you' anymore.
I say, 'Help me up!' "

DOPE: What makes you think your wife is getting tired of you?
DOPIER: She keeps wrapping my lunch in a road map!

A businessman was suddenly notified that he must immediately come to a big conference in his Chicago office. It was scheduled to last a week and he had to take a plane at LaGuardia in an hour.

Suddenly he remembered that he would not be able to reach his wife by phone to tell her of the change in his plans, as she was out shopping for clothes for a trip to Europe.

The man thought hard for a moment, then telephoned his secretary. He told her to telephone all stores and cancel all of his wife's charge accounts. She called him at his office in a positive fury, fifteen minutes later.

•

A housewife who devoted most of her life to spending twice as much as her husband earned complained constantly about the apartment they lived in. "All our friends live ten times better than we do," was her chorus. "We simply must move into a more expensive neighborhood." One night her long-suffering spouse came home and told her, "Well, we won't have to move after all. The landlord just doubled our rent."

•

The new maid—a fresh little country girl—picked up the phone, muttered something, and slammed it down again.

"Who was it, Betsy?" the man of the house asked eagerly. "I'm expecting an important long-distance call."

"Only some mad idiot, Mr. Thorpe," she answered. "He said it was a long distance from California. I told him we knew it was!"

A newly installed housewife who had just moved into a new town greeted the mailman her first morning in the new house and asked his name.

"Frank Sinatra," he replied.

"My, *that's* a well-known name!" she exclaimed.

"Should be," he grunted. "Been delivering mail in this neighborhood for almost thirty years."

•

"Mary," the housewife said severely to the new maid, "I can write my name on the dust on the piano!"

"Oh, ma'am," marveled the maid, "what a grand thing it is to have an education!"

•

When a woman in a pleasant suburban town went on vacation one summer, she let her cook have hers at the same time, leaving her husband to get his meals in a restaurant.

Before departing the cook put out all the empty milk bottles with this note:

"Please don't leave no more milk. The lady of the house is away, and the gentleman, he drinks out."

•

"Why, George!" a surprised wife exclaimed to her husband. "Why are you taking a suitcase with you this morning? Are you going away?"

"No," the husband replied. "But I heard you talking about the church giving a rummage sale, so I'm taking my clothes down to the office, where they'll be safe until it's over."

26 •

A widow had a séance with a spiritualist medium who in the course of a few moments of deep concentration and hoarse breathing told her that her late husband was there and she could converse with him. It was a tense moment.

"Dear John, are you happy there?" she began. "*Very* happy," he assured her.

"Happier than you were here with me?"

"Oh my yes, *much* happier."

"John dear, what is Heaven like?"

"I don't know dear, I didn't get there!"

Two men were confiding the secrets of their happy marriages.

MIKE: Don't you two ever have a difference of opinion?

SPIKE: Oh yes indeed. But I never tell her about them. And you, what's your secret?

MIKE: Well, we've arranged that *she* makes all the minor decisions and *I* make all the important ones.

SPIKE: Which ones do *you* make, then?

MIKE: Oh, such things as whether to adopt Esperanto as an international language, whether to admit China to the United Nations, and if women should have the vote in Switzerland.

•

A demonstration of hypnosis was being given at a large private party. A man volunteered as a subject and, after he had been put into a trance, the hypnotist told him he could type.

A machine was produced and, to everyone's surprise, the man did an expert typing job although he had never even tried it before.

The hypnotist then asked him to write a letter to the girl he loved best. When it was finished, he read it to the assembled guests:

"Dearest Jeanne," it said. "I love you terribly and can hardly wait until tomorrow when I can see you again."

There was a sudden stir in the room, and an indignant woman rushed out the door. The hypnotist brought the man out of his trance. He glanced about the room and called out to his wife:

"Anne, Anne, where *are* you, darling?"

A young father was wheeling his baby son's carriage through the park. The son was screaming with rage, but the man was merely repeating softly:

"Control yourself, Egbert. Just remain calm, Egbert."

A child psychologist, sunning on a park bench, observed the scene approvingly, then tapped the young father on the shoulder. "You control your temper admirably, my friend," he said warmly. "So he's named Egbert, eh?"

"Not at all," corrected the father. "He's named Herbert, I'm Egbert."

The wife and children went off on a vacation and the man found that they'd taken the only key to the mailbox. So he phoned her—and she mailed him the key.

A busy mother with seven children hired a girl to help out, but found that her one failing was oversleeping in the morning.

"I must warn you, Betsy," the mother said, "that every time we have to cook breakfast ourselves I'll deduct a dollar from your salary."

Betsy tried. But a few mornings later she shuffled down from her room long after the children had left for school.

"Betsy, we had to get our own breakfast again."

"Well, yes, ma'am," the girl agreed. "But I'm paying you for it, aren't I?"

•

DANNY: Can you bake an apple pie the way my mother used to bake them?

FANNY: Not unless your mother was my domestic science teacher.

•

"I'm always doing the wrong thing," moaned the young bride the morning after her first big party. "Last night one of our guests started to tell a naughty story, and I told him he could just get his hat and go home."

"A little drastic perhaps," her friend agreed. "But your heart was in the right place, anyway. What happened?"

"Most of the other guests went *with* him—to hear the rest of the story!"

•

CONSCIENTIOUS CLARA: Dear, are we supposed to write our congressman twice a year, or do I have it mixed up with seeing our dentist?

MRS. BEREFT: My husband went out six months ago for a loaf of bread and never came back. What should I do?
SYMPATHETIC NEIGHBOR: Well, if I were you, I wouldn't wait any longer. I'd send one of the children out for the loaf of bread.

•

WEARY WINIFRED: My husband bought me a new spring outfit: a spade, a rake, and ten packets of seeds!

•

Gloomy Gus, while writing out checks for the monthly bills: Well, we're *at* the bridge we were going to cross when we came to it.

Enigmatic Epigrams

HORACE: What is it that you can't see that's always before you?
MORRIS: The future.

•

HARRY: Why is a balloon like a beggar?
LARRY: Because it has no visible means of support.

•

WISE WILFRED: A neighbor's child is something that stands halfway between an adult and a television screen.

DINER: Where's the chicken in this chicken pie?
WAITER: Would you expect to find a dog in a dog biscuit?

WISE WILLIE: The trouble with a lot of us is that in trying times we stop trying.

•

RANDY: Why does a music teacher have to be a good teacher?
SANDY: Because she's a sound instructor.

•

A wise Irishman says: "The leprechauns and the fairies are going; the magnates and the tycoons are coming. But there are still a few thoughtful people who prefer the Little People to the Big People."

•

Dumb Dora figures it out: a raisin is a worried grape.

•

Uncle Ebenezer says that punctuality is something that, if you have it, there usually isn't anybody around to appreciate it.

•

MRS. GUSH: A howling success is a baby that gets picked up.

•

ARNIE: Why is a nobleman like a book?
BARNIE: Because he has a title.

•

Bored Bess says lazily, the people who keep saying they hope they're not intruding always are.

DUMB DORA: How many big men are born in this world?
BRIGHT BETTY: None. Only small babies are born.

•

LOUIE: What is the most dangerous vegetable to have on a yacht?
STUIE: A leek.

•

ANDY: What bird is present at every meal?
SANDY: The swallow.

•

FRANK: What makes the tower of Pisa lean?
HANK: It never eats.

•

DORA: What books should be kept on top of the shelf?
CORA: Tall stories.

•

MRS. POORE: What is it about coffee that keeps you awake?
MR. POORE: The high price.

•

Q: Why is a heart of a tree like a dog's tail?
A: It is farthest from the bark.

•

SMART: What kind paper should I use when I make my kite?
ALECK: Flypaper.

34 •

Mr. Fussbudget complains that summer is the time of year when the highway authorities close the throughways and open up the detours.

BENNY: Why isn't your nose twelve inches long?
LENNY: If it was, it would be a foot.

•

CYNICAL CLAUDE: To love and win is the best thing. To love and lose is the next best.

•

Mrs. Chatter confides: A secret is something you tell to only one person at a time.

•

DAPPER DAN: A gourmet is a glutton with a dinner jacket.

HUGHIE: What room has no walls, doors, or floors?
LOUIE: A mushroom.

•

SAM SOUR: Waiter, what do you call this dish?
WAITER: A mixed grill, sir.
SAM SOUR: Mixed?
WAITER: Yes, sir. Some of it's good, and some of it's bad.

OLD OTTO: As you get older you find that the best time for a cold shower is some other time.

•

Sage Sally, learning to ice-skate: Success is getting up just one more time than you fall.

•

Mayor Moppus has discovered that "alimony is when two people make a mistake and one person pays for it."

Foreign Foibles

A Texan had worked himself up from a field hand and was now one of the richest men in the state. One summer he treated himself to a trip to Europe.

When he arrived at an Irish hotel in the middle of a blazing June day the manager was very puzzled to see the skis, snowshoes, toboggans, and winter sports equipment his chauffeur brought in from his Cadillac.

"Pardon me, sir," said the manager apologetically, "but you surely must know we have no snow in Galway at this time of the year."

The tycoon waved the problem away with his hand. "Don't worry about it. We're having the snow sent on later with the heavy luggage."

•

An English secretary hadn't worked very long for her New York boss when he had to make a quick trip to London.

Soon after he left, there was a call from California. The new secretary asked if the caller wished to speak to someone else, as her boss was in the United Kingdom.

There was a long pause on the other end of the line. Then the man's voice blurted out:

"This is terrible! Is it too late to send flowers?"

An American couple strolled along the banks of the
Seine, under the shadows of Notre Dame. He was lost in
silence. She said, finally:

"What are you thinking about, darling?"

"I was thinking, dear, that if anything happened to
either of us, I'd like to spend the rest of my life in Paris."

A spry old gentleman of eighty-five enjoyed traveling by air when he visited any of his many children. On one trip his son met him at the airport and, surprised to see the old man carrying a cane, exclaimed, "Dad, I didn't know you needed to walk with a cane now."

"I don't," his father said with a sly wink. "But I get more attention from the stewardesses this way!"

•

The visitor complained of the long muddy road to the hotel that could be traveled only on foot.

"Well now," soothed the proprietor, "if it was any shorter, it wouldn't reach the house."

•

An Irish-American went back to the old country and celebrated a bit too much one evening with his old buddies. On the way home he lost his way, drove his car right into an old cottage on the road to Cork, and drew up neatly beside the fireplace. He leaned out and spoke to the old lady sitting in the armchair.

"Shay, ish this the road to Dublin?"

She shook her head, and smiled sweetly. "No, sir. You'll have to turn left over there by the piano and keep straight ahead when you pass the kitchen table."

•

On another one of his stops, the same man went on to tell, the cooking wasn't bad. "On the first day we were there one of the chickens died and we had chicken soup. The next day one of the pigs died, and we had pork chops. Then the landlady's husband died, so we left."

Daniel Dandy returned from a trip to Paris and a friend asked him how he'd liked it.

"Wonderful!" said Daniel. "Only I wish I could have made the trip twenty years ago."

"You mean when Paris was really Paris?"

"No, I mean when Daniel Dandy was really Daniel Dandy!"

•

SMART ALECK: In the United States coffee breaks slow up industrial production; in England it's called absent-tea-ism.

•

An old Scottish guide returned from taking the new minister on a grouse-shooting trip over the moors and sank wearily into his chair before the fire.

"Here's a cup of hot tea for you, Angus," said his wife. "And is the new minister a good shot?"

The old fellow puffed his pipe a bit, then he replied, "Aye, a fine shot he is. But 'tis marvelous indeed how the Lord protects the birds when he's shooting!"

A traveler was journeying to an out-of-the-way village in England to visit an old schoolmate. When the slow train finally arrived, he found himself in front of a little wooden station in the middle of a field, with scarcely a building in sight.

"Why in the name of Heaven," he asked wearily, "did they build the railway station three miles from the village?"

"Well, sir," said the stationmaster, "it was thought that it would be a good thing to have the station near the trains."

•

Reporting on a trip to a rather primitive country, an American diplomat related that on one of his stops he had stayed at what was really not a bad hotel—and it was truly inexpensive: the proprietor said that the room would cost only $3 a night if the diplomat was willing to make his own bed.

"I said I would," the diplomat went on, "and he gave me a hammer and nails and an armload of two-by-fours!"

•

There are still parts of Ireland where, to make an understatement, the train service isn't as good as it should be. On one occasion a tourist complained bitterly of the slowness of the train.

"Why then," asked the conductor, "don't you get off and walk?"

"Well, I'm not in *that* much of a hurry," the tourist demurred.

A Londoner wanted to return to an Irish farm where he had spent a previous vacation, but he wrote first to say that he had been annoyed by the noisy squealing of the pigs the first time.

The farmer replied by return mail: "Don't worry at all. We haven't had a pig since you were here."

Romantic Ray met Romantic Kay on a train, and the encounter proved to be a most romantic one.

As they chugged toward a mountain he remarked, "We're coming to a tunnel. Are you afraid?"

"No," she said. "Not if you take that cigar out of your mouth."

Goofy Girls

"Oh, my new boyfriend is *ever* so romantic!" Dorothea rhapsodized to her girl friend. "Every time he speaks to me he addresses me as 'Fair Lady.'"

"That's just force of habit," replied her friend. "He used to be a bus conductor."

•

MAISIE: I caught my boyfriend flirting.
DAISY: I caught mine that way, too.

•

He and she were having a romantic tryst beside the lake in the park.
HE: If I married you, Marie, would your father give you a handsome wedding present?
SHE: Yes, Bob.
HE: And do you think he'd let us live with him in his big house if we got married?
SHE: Yes, Bob.
HE: And would he take me into his business and let me rise rapidly to the top?
SHE: Yes, Bob.
HE: Will you marry me, Marie?
SHE: No, Bob.

Kitty was an expert knitter and she was always looking for unusual patterns to use on sweaters.

One evening while eating in a Chinese restaurant she was entranced with the Chinese characters opposite one of the entrees on the menu. She took the menu home and the result, several weeks later, was a stunning black sweater with the Chinese characters running from shoulder to waist.

She wore it one day when she met a friend who knew Chinese. He burst into roars of laughter, and then translated for her what she had so skillfully worked in wool:

"This dish is cheap but most delicious."

Cynical Cathy says that men hope that their lean years are behind them. But women hope that theirs are ahead.

Flirty Flo says a clever girl judges the sparkle and shine a shampoo puts in her hair by checking the sparkle and shine in her date's eyes.

•

After struggling, without success, to follow the directions for installing a wall-type can opener, the housewife gave up and made herself a pot of tea to soothe her nerves.

When she returned, the opener was neatly in place, and the cleaning woman was already using it.

"How in the world did you do it?" she said in wondering admiration.

"Well, ma'am," was the reply, "when you can't read, you've just got to think."

•

Romantic Rena says that young girls who think only of boys quickly outgrow such juvenile foolishness and begin to think about *men.*

•

Mrs. Strict and her maid failed to agree about various problems around the house, and finally Mrs. Strict fired the girl. Later, feeling a bit conscience-stricken, she tried to smooth things over a little.

"Nora," she said, as the girl was about to leave, "I would like to give you a good letter of reference, but I can't. For one thing, you never *did* have our meals ready on time. Now, I wonder if you can tell me how I can write *that* down in a nice way?"

"Well," retorted Nora nonchalantly, "you might write down that I got the meals the same way I got my pay!"

FIRST FARMER: I wish I had my wife back.

SECOND FARMER: Where is she?

FIRST FARMER: I traded her for a team of draft horses.

SECOND FARMER: And now you realize how much you love her?

FIRST FARMER: No, now I need a wagon.

•

A pleasant, plumpish woman was trying on a new dress in a department store. She thought it looked all right in the front, but had some doubts about the way it fitted in the back, where she couldn't see it too well in the mirror.

"Tell me honestly," she said to the salesgirl. "Is this dress big enough for me?"

"Well, honey," the girl said, "if you mean coming, the dress is made for you. Going, you could use a size larger."

FATHER: So my daughter has consented to become your wife. Have you fixed the day of the wedding?
GROOM-TO-BE: I will leave that to my fiancée.
FATHER: And will you have a church or a private wedding?
GROOM: Her mother will decide that, sir.
FATHER: What will you have to live on?
GROOM: I will leave that entirely to you, sir.

•

Silly Dilly avers: I like men who make things. Like Mr. Newgilt. He made $100,000 last year.

•

A mother reports that as she was helping her blissful teen-age daughter get ready for her first formal dance, the girl turned to her and asked,

"Mother, did they have parties like this when you were alive?"

•

The landlady wanted to please her new lodger, and the first day she gave him two slices of bread for his lunch box. He didn't seem satisfied, so she gave him four slices the next day, and then six slices, and so on until he was getting ten.

Even then he acted as if it wasn't enough and so, in despair, she cut the loaf in half and put a huge slab of ham between the pieces. When he came in that evening, she asked:

"Was there enough in your lunch today?"

"It wasn't bad," he said grudgingly, "but I see you're back to the two slices again."

Sue was about to go out on her first real date and she asked her mother:

"What shall I do if he tries to kiss me good-night?"

"Well," said her understanding mother, "I suppose you could whisper for help."

•

Dopey Diana, trying to impress the visiting author: You know, I read a couple of paragraphs of your book every night to put myself to sleep!

•

A wealthy matron hired a new maid just a day before an important dinner party and instructed her carefully on how to wait on table.

"Now do remember, Mary, always serve from the left and remove the plates from the right. Do you understand?"

"Yes, ma'am. You people *are* superstitious, aren't you!"

Tired husband, arriving home from work: "I've made up my mind to stay home this evening, darling."

"Too late, Harry," his loving spouse trilled. "I've made up my face to go out."

•

Dolorous Dolly complains that her illnesses are so rare that there aren't any symptoms.

•

Philosophical Phyllis says she has finally learned three rather discouraging things about men:

One—they went to war and killed each other when, if only they would be patient, they'd all die a natural death.

Two—they climbed trees and knocked down apples when, if they'd only be patient, the apples would fall to the ground.

Three—they pursued women when, if they'd only be patient, women would pursue them.

SALLY SHOPPER: Can I wear this fur in the rain without ruining it?
SALESGIRL: Have you ever seen a beaver carrying an umbrella?

•

A woman came into a very chic store and tried on twenty dresses—and nothing, but nothing, suited her. Finally, she said, "I think all of these are too tailored—I would look better in something flowing." The weary salesgirl agreed and told her to go jump in the river.

•

Sophisticated Susanne says that adolescence is when a girl begins to powder and a boy begins to puff.

Hilarious Homilies

A famous actor says that his grandfather was, by his definition, a true gentleman: one day when they were walking down the street, they encountered an old beggar with a sign saying:

I AM BLIND.

The grandfather gave the boy a coin, which he dropped into the beggar's cup, and then scolded him afterward because he hadn't raised his hat as he did so.

"You must always be polite to your elders," the old man said.

"But he was *blind*. He *couldn't* have seen me raise my hat."

"He might be a fraud," replied his grandfather.

•

The late Christopher Morley once said, "If we discovered that we had only five minutes left to say all we wanted to say, every phone booth would be occupied by people saying, 'I love you.'"

•

Contrary Carl was summoned for jury duty. Afterward he told friends that he'd done a good job despite "eleven of the most stupid, stubborn people" he'd ever met in his life.

A young bride went to visit her husband's mother and was impressed by her delicious molasses cookies. She asked for the recipe. The older woman told her all the ingredients, ending with: "Molasses, four gallups."

"Four *what?*" asked the bride.

"*You* know—tip the molasses jug till it says 'gallup'—and do it four times," replied the old woman matter-of-factly.

•

A young actor asked a great star how he came to be so much of a success.

"Easy," replied the star. "All you have to do is get applause when you come on and applause when you go off."

A tortoise once challenged a hare to a race.

"You must be crazy!" declared the hare.

"I *am* a little stupid," admitted the tortoise, "but I've always yearned to be a great athlete. . . . Oh, I know it sounds crazy," he added, a bit apologetically.

"Okay! Okay! I'll race you, I'll run you right into the ground!" shouted the hare.

He covered half the course before the tortoise was well started, but then he felt a little silly at having such an easy victory, so he lay down for a while. When the tortoise finally padded into view, the hare was fast asleep.

The tortoise kept going, but almost immediately *his* conscience began to bother *him*. He remembered an old folk saying from one of his school books that had impressed him—something to the effect that it did not matter whether you won or lost, so much as *how* you played the game.

So he turned around and went back, poking the hare softly with his nose to wake him. The startled and confused hare leaped up and raced off instantly in the direction the tortoise was pointed, toward the starting line. And the tortoise turned slowly around again and plodded on to victory.

Moral: Nice guys don't always finish last!

A Scotsman bought a car for very little money. Several days later a friend asked him how it was going.

"Och," replied the Scotsman. "I'm just beginning to realize how hard it is to drive a bargain!"

Motherly Molly has finally decided that babies are notoriously the most greedy, egocentric, ruthless, and grasping of beings. Even while they're being tenderly petted they're plotting to snatch your eyeglasses, grab your watch, swallow a safety pin, and bite off one of their toes. "But they are *irresistible!*" she always ends by saying.

•

Sour Sarah says a good listener is usually thinking about something else.

The sign on the farmer's gate read:

"No Help Wanted. The man who planted, fertilized, pruned, weeded, and worried over this fruit also prefers to pick it himself. . . . But thanks anyway."

GENERAL: I am a firm believer in fighting the enemy with his own weapons.

CIVILIAN: How long does it take you to sting a bee?

•

Happy Hannah says that a good marriage is when a woman gives the best years of her life to the man who *made* them the best.

SMART SAUL: Misers aren't much fun to live with, but they make wonderful ancestors!

•

Sir Winston Churchill once said that an appeaser is one who feeds a crocodile—hoping it will eat him last.

Motherly Molly says sadly that a mother's life is a contradiction: first she worries that some designing female will carry off her son—then that no designing male will carry off her daughter.

•

Dolorous Don says that when it comes time "for the meek to inherit the earth," taxes will be so high they won't want it.

•

SAGE SAM: Women think that having children makes them mothers. That's like saying that having a piano makes them musicians!

The efficiency expert watched the old man sawing wood in his back yard and walked over to have a word with him.

THE EXPERT: You know, you could saw twice as much wood if you got an electric saw.

OLD MAN: Sure. But I don't need twice as much wood.

●

SALESMAN: That chair is worth $5,000.

CUSTOMER: How could it possibly be worth that much?

SALESMAN: That's what it cost me last year sitting in it instead of going out after business.

●

Broke Billy says sadly the only thing left to tax these days is the wolf at the door.

The ambitious woman who had put all her life savings into a quite elegant dress shop was delighted the first morning to see the door open to admit her first customer.

Remembering how important an impression of business was, she quickly seized the telephone and began a conversation with, supposedly, another customer. She named a time for her imaginary customer to come for a fitting, said good-bye, then turned to the patiently waiting man.

"And what can I do for you, sir?" she said in a refined tone.

"If you please, ma'am, I've come to connect the telephone!"

•

MINISTER: The beauty of the Bible is unsurpassed.
PARISHIONER: But what good is beauty if you can't understand it?
MINISTER: Well, twenty-five years ago I married a beautiful woman. I still don't understand her, but I have no desire to replace her with a plainer one.

•

HARRY (somewhat pompously): I believe one should do something every day to make other people happy.
LARRY (somewhat slyly): Like leaving them alone?

Mrs. Manykids says that to discipline boys successfully, you must start at the bottom.

A Scottish farmer was reading his evening paper when his hired man came in to tell him that there was a strange cow in the pasture. "What'll I do with her?" he asked.

"What a silly question," said the Scotsman. "Milk her and turn 'er oot."

•

"It's strange," said the old man, "how afraid young men are, nowadays, to marry and settle down. They actually seem to *fear* marriage. . . . Why, before I was married, I didn't know the meaning of fear!"

•

Educated Eddie warns that horse sense is usually found in a stable mind.

Instant Insanity

Miss Heiress bought her fiancé a stunningly handsome and expensive yacht for a Christmas surprise. As the salesman was writing out the sales check, she gaily instructed him, "Now you be sure to wrap it so he can't guess what it is!"

•

Gus was a pretty good golfer, but he never came in under par because of the hangup he had about the hole with the gully.

On one bright Saturday morning he came to that dread number twelve and said to his caddy, "Well, here I go, straight into the gully again!"

"Not today, sir," said the caddy. "They've filled it in."

Gus made a beautiful drive right onto the green. Then he walked down the course and came to the same old gully. "But you said . . ." He looked at the caddy.

"Sure. But I was talking to my head-shrinker about you and he gave me an idea. I figured if you thought it wasn't there, you wouldn't go into it."

•

RENA: Where's the best place to put a bathroom scale?
RONA: In front of the refrigerator.

Mrs. Elegante strode confidently into the small town's best butcher shop, informed the butcher that she was a newcomer in town—that she and her husband had bought the Vanderhouse mansion in Beauville Heights, that they had moved there from Park Avenue in New York, "and," she told him somewhat severely, "we are used to the *very best*."

"And now, my good man," she said to the somewhat overwhelmed owner of the shop, "I want two dozen of your top lamb chops. Be sure you make them lean!" she warned.

"Yes, ma'am," he replied. "To the left or the right?"

●

SALLY: My sister is very stubborn.
SILLY: In what way?
SALLY: I can never convince her I'm right when she knows I'm wrong.

The journalist asked the returned war general, "Did you have any horses in that theater of action, sir?"

"We did indeed," replied the general.

"And how were they?"

"Tasty, very tasty," said the general.

•

SMART: Three men fell out into the water, but only two got their hair wet.

ALECK: Why?

SMART: One of them was bald.

The manager of a golf club was hiring a new partner.

"Now then, what do they call you?"

"Douglas Denby," replied the newcomer.

"You should say 'Sir'!" snapped the manager.

"Okay. *Sir* Douglas Denby."

•

Mr. Brown said to his neighbor at a business banquet, "You didn't laugh at Harper's joke. How come? *I* thought it was hilarious."

"It was a good one," agreed his neighbor. "But I don't like Harper. I'll laugh when I get home."

IRK: What did the moon boy say to the moon girl? JERK: Let's take a stroll. There's a beautiful earth out tonight.

The athletic hero was a terrible bore. The girls had a hard time listening to him at parties.

One evening, after he'd told his date about all his achievements in football and baseball, he began to tell her how he planned to do great things in track.

"And next," he said confidently, "I'm going to run the mile."

The girl suddenly sparkled with interest. "When," she asked, "do you start?"

•

One day, going down in the apartment house elevator, Dizzy Liz met her neighbor carrying a covered birdcage. "What's in that?" she asked.

"My pet rooster," he replied.

She fainted. When she came to, she moaned softly, "And to think that I've been paying a psychiatrist fifty dollars a week for a year because I kept thinking I heard a rooster crowing!"

PAUL: What's your cat's name?

MOLL: Ben Hur.

PAUL: How did you happen to call it *that*?

MOLL: Well, we used to call it Ben—until it had kittens!

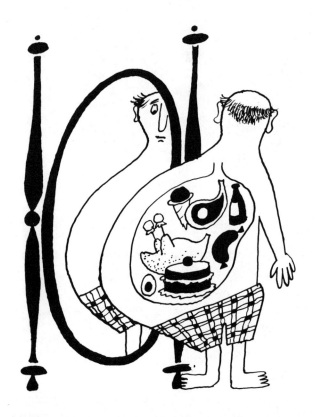

FATSO: Where's all that grocery money that I give you?

FLORA: Stand sideways and look in the mirror.

•

The ad read: "With this new paste, women with copper bottoms will no longer have any trouble keeping them shining like new."

64 •

The classified ad was quite explicit:

LION TAMER WANTS TAMER LION.

The thunder god went for a ride
Upon his favorite filly.
"I'm Thor," he cried.
The horse replied,
"Thor, you forgot your thaddle, thilly!"

A teen-age young man took his first date to Coney Island amusement park. They headed straight for the Tunnel of Love.

But the next day the boy told his friends about his disappointment with this experience. "It was dark and scary. Besides, we got soaking wet."

"Why?" they asked. "Did the boat leak?"

"You mean there's a *boat*?"

LORA: What did the envelope say to the stamp?
DORA: You may be square, but you sure do send me!

•

Neighboring apartment dwellers met in the lobby one morning. Said one, "Look, old man, didn't you hear me knocking on the wall last night?"

"Oh, that's all right," replied the other, blearily, "think nothing of it—*we* were making quite a bit of noise ourselves."

BOSS: Did you mark this crate Fragile—This Side Up?
FUZZY FRITZ: Yes, sir, like you told me. In fact, to make real sure of it, I marked it that way on all four sides!

•

A British newspaper reported recently: "The duchess smashed the bottle of champagne against the bow of the ship, and amid the cheers of the crowd she slid on her greasy bottom into the sea."

•

The city boy was to work on a farm for the summer. The evening he arrived, he ate a big supper and went to bed early. The next thing he knew, the farmer was shaking him and saying, "It's four-thirty!"

"Well, gosh, sir, you'd better go to bed now," muttered the city boy sleepily. "You must have a lot of work to do tomorrow!"

GOLFER: Tell me, caddie, why do you keep looking at your watch?
CADDIE: This is no watch, sir, this is a compass!

•

Two leopards finished their dinner, and one of them leaned back and sighed with satisfaction:
"That just hit the right spots!"

•

VISITOR, to guide: The sky seems to be much clearer here in New York City.
GUIDE: It is! It's because we have skyscrapers.

•

GOLFER: I've *never* played this badly before.
CADDIE: You mean you've played *before*?

•

TOURIST: How long does winter last here in Alaska?
OLD-TIMER: Every year since I've been around, it's lasted thirteen months!

•

TEACHER IN POETRY APPRECIATION CLASS: "Gentle zephyr, come from heaven." Randolph, what does "zephyr" mean?
CITY BOY: Please, ma'am, a young cow.

•

BOB: My wife talks to herself all the time.
ROB: So does mine, but she doesn't know it. She thinks I'm listening.

PASSENGER (climbing on to the crosstown bus): Do you stop at the East River?

DRIVER: If I don't, sir, there'll be one heck of a splash!

Job Jests

A busy executive was in the habit of having his secretary phone down to the local coffee shop for a sandwich for lunch. After years of this routine, he wearied of the same old list—liverwurst-on-rye, bacon-lettuce-tomato, roast-beef, and all the rest. One day he decided to invent a new taste sensation.

"Make it a pastrami and peanut butter with anchovies and raw onion," he said to the astonished girl.

Obediently, she phoned in the order. The executive liked it so much he repeated it every day for weeks.

One day, hurrying back to his office just before lunchtime, he stopped in the coffee shop downstairs and said to the girl at the counter, "A pastrami with peanut butter and anchovies and raw onion to go, please."

The girl's mouth dropped open. Then, after a moment's take, she swung around and called out to the chef in the back, "Ben! It's *him*! Come and look!"

•

Sally Spinster has some pretty sound ideas. "Why do you suppose it is," she says wisely, "that thousands of girls are longing for a man who will free them from seven hours in an office—so that they can slave for fourteen hours in a house?"

SALESMAN: What do you do with all those apples?
FARMER: We can eat all we can, and what we can't we can.
SALESMAN: We sell what we can sell, and what we can't sell we cancel.

•

A Toronto paper ran this ad, which got answers from a score of girls:

"Clerk-Typist for Plumbers and Steamfitters Union. You'll have to work like crazy, there are no benefits—but an opportunity to meet two thousand men."

The office boy was forever late and very inventive at thinking up excuses for it.

"Well, what happened *this* time?" asked the boss wearily.

"I fell out of a penthouse window," the lad said quickly.

"It doesn't seem to have hurt you any."

"No," the boy said. "The ground broke my fall."

•

Two men worked side by side in a very large organization employing hundreds of people. One of them always went home on the stroke of five; the other often worked until seven or later, trying to clear his desk.

One day when they met at the water cooler, the harder worker asked the other, "Do you mind telling he how you manage to clean off your desk by five every day?"

"Very simple," replied the other. "When a difficult or tiresome problem is sent over to me I just mark it, 'Refer to J. Smith.' I figure that in an outfit as big as this one there's *bound* to be a J. Smith."

"There is," said his co-worker, eyeing him malevolently. "*I* am J. Smith."

•

An immigrant husband, home from his first day of work in America, attempted to describe his job to his inquisitive wife: "I work on an assembly line with three other fellows. When a car comes down the line, the first fellow puts on the bolt, the second attaches the washer, and the third holds the bolt and washer in place. . . ."

"Yes," the wife said impatiently, "but what do *you* do?"

"Me," he said proudly, "I screw up the works!"

The Chamber of Commerce gathered one day at lunch to honor the seventy-fifth anniversary of one of the town's leading manufacturers. After a very laudatory speech the master of ceremonies said to the assemblage:

"This is a great and noble occasion: seventy-five years is a very long time. Is there anyone else present who represents a concern that has been in existence that long?"

A minister rose and said quietly, "I have that honor, sir."

The ad read: "The Presbyterian Church requires the services of an organist and choir director, either male or female."

One of the replies read: "I notice that you have a vacancy for an organist and choirmaster, either lady or gentleman. Having been both for several years, I beg to apply for the position."

A newly commissioned second lieutenant found himself without change in front of a cigarette machine. He flagged down a passing private and asked, "Got change of a dollar?"

"I think so," the private replied cheerfully. "Let me see."

The lieutenant stiffened at the private's casual manner and barked, "Private, that is not the way to address an officer! Let's try it again. Got change of a dollar?"

The private came to attention, saluted smartly, and said, "No, sir."

The young girl eagerly approached her first day on her first job, but was soon disheartened by the typist at the next desk.

"It's a wonderful office," said the latter, "once you've resigned yourself to the fact that there's no chance here for advancement, a raise, or marriage."

•

Ambitious Al placed this ad in the newspaper:

"Mr. Alston will be at Harper's barbershop, starting Sunday, and states that he is again available for butchering livestock."

But he was outdone by another ad run in the same edition:

"Wanted: Smart young man for butcher's. Able to cut, skewer, and serve a customer."

•

PHIL: Why did you become a printer?
BILL: Oh, I guess I just seemed the right type.

PAT: What is your job at the watch factory?
MAT: I sit there and make faces.

The boss was a basically kindhearted man who liked to help young people. After a five-month trial he called in the new employee.

"Robert," he said, "I'm going to give you an opportunity to make something of yourself. . . . You're fired."

•

Parson Drake phoned the local board of health to ask that a dead mule be removed from the front of his house.

"I thought you ministers took care of the dead," said the clerk.

"We do," answered the parson, "but first we get in touch with the relatives."

•

The traveling salesman handed his expense account over to the head bookkeeper, who examined it for a few minutes and then said, "How in the name of heaven can you spend twenty-five dollars a day for meals in Kalamazoo?"

"Easy," answered the salesman cheerfully. "I always skip breakfast."

76 •

STERN WIFE: Well, did you ask for that raise today?
MEEK HUSBAND, sighing: No, dear. I'm afraid I forgot it again, in the excitement of getting fired.

•

Earnest Ernest advises that perseverance is getting on with the job when you know it's impossible.

•

One day, the coffee-dispensing machine came up with some very pretty new cups. Upon draining the cups, the office crew found printed on the inside of each one: "Get back to work now."

•

A couple of bone-tired salesclerks were locking up their cash registers after a rough day dealing with the Christmas shoppers.

Suddenly the closing bell sounded.

"Listen!" One girl turned eagerly to the other. "They're playing *our* song!"

•

A traveling salesman was stranded in the Midwest by a blizzard that caused all transportation to grind to a halt. He wired his boss for instructions.

The reply came back within hours: "Start summer vacation immediately."

•

Uncle Ebenezer counsels, "The prime of life is when the elevator boy calls you 'Sir' and the boss calls you 'Son.'"

The office manager, at a staff meeting, said in a severe tone, "Things are getting just a little too relaxed around here. From now on, no one goes home a minute before closing time!—unless the boss leaves early."

•

Personnel manager: "Aren't you the same boy who applied for a job a week ago?"

"Yes, sir."

"Well, I told you then that I wanted an older boy."

"I know, sir. That's why I've come back now. I had a birthday yesterday."

Kute Kids

Wise Winifred returned from summer camp with awards for woodcraft, hiking, and sailing—and also with a small star.

Asked what the star was for, she replied, "For having my trunk packed neatly when we came home."

Her mother was very pleased until Winifred added, "I hadn't unpacked it."

•

The family moved from the country to the city, and his mother gave little Bobby careful instructions about traffic.

"Never cross the street until the cars have passed," she said, as he started off to visit a little friend.

About an hour later he returned, his eyes brimming with tears.

"What's happened?" his mother asked in alarm.

"I couldn't go," said Bobby. "I waited and waited, but a car never *did* come by!"

•

Silly Sally wrote an essay in class; it was entitled "My Family."

"In my family there are three people—my father, my mother, and me," it began. "I am the youngest."

The teacher noticed three little boys sitting on the school steps at recess. One had a toy spaceship, the second a toy car, and the third a copy of a quite adult humorous men's magazine.

"What would you like to be, son?" he asked the first boy.

"An astronaut," was the reply.

"And you?" he said to the second boy.

"A racing driver, sir."

"And what would *you* like to be?" he asked the one with the rather racy magazine.

The boy dragged his eyes away from the glossy pages and replied fervently:

"Grown, sir, grown!"

•

ROMANTIC RENA: Heaven must be a very beautiful place because even the wrong side of it is so pretty.

•

A little girl rushed home from her first symphony concert and reported breathlessly to her family:

"They played Beethoven's Fifth. It was beautiful! I wouldn't change a note of it!"

Despite the best efforts of child psychiatrists, there are still a lot of kids of four or five—even in sophisticated New York—who believe in Santa Claus.

One of them was taken by his mother to the toy department in Macy's on a December morning last year and was duly propped up on Santa's lap.

"What do you want for Christmas, my lad?" asked Santa Claus dutifully.

"Better write it down," said the lad, "or you'll forget."

"Trust me," urged Santa. "My memory never fails."

The lad was dubious, but catalogued his demands.

The same afternoon, mother and son arrived at Gimbels and the lad found himself on Santa's lap for a second time. The Gimbels Santa asked the usual question: "What do you want for Christmas?"

The lad slipped off his lap, kicked him lustily in the shin, and yelled, "You numbskull, I *knew* you'd forget!"

A dapper New Yorker—one of the ten best-dressed men in America—came to collect his six-year-old daughter at a birthday party. Taking hold of her hand to guide her across the street, he observed, "Goodness, Vicki, your hands seem mighty sticky today."

"Yours would be too," she informed him, "if you had a piece of lemon pie and a chocolate eclair inside your muff."

•

Little Sally spent the day in bed with a cold and drove her mother almost frantic with requests for crayons, ice cream, her favorite toys, glasses of water, and storytelling.

At last her weary mother decided to ignore Sally for a while so that she could prepare dinner.

After half an hour Mother became a bit alarmed. Not a sound from Sally's room. She tiptoed to the doorway and peeked in, hoping the patient had finally fallen asleep. Sally was not asleep. She was fuming.

"Don't bother coming now," she said coldly. "I've died."

•

LITTLE OLD LADY: Goodness, sonny—why are you paddling with your socks on?

LITTLE BOY: Well, the water's cold at this time of the year.

Mother and Millie were in the kitchen washing the dishes; Daddy and Danny were in the living room watching television. Suddenly there was a crash of falling dishes. Daddy and Danny listened, but heard nothing more.

"It was Mother who dropped them," Danny announced finally.

"How do you know?"

"Because she isn't saying anything."

•

HANK: Live dangerously!

FRANK: Is there any other way?

•

"Grandpa, why don't you get a hearing aid?"

"Don't need it, son. I hear more now than I can understand."

Young Judy wrote home from her first time at summer camp:

"The first day I didn't have any friends. The second day I had several friends. The third day I had both friends and enemies."

•

Jimmy went shopping for his mother's birthday present.

"I'd like to see some cookie jars, please," he asked the salesgirl.

She showed him a variety of pretty jars and he carefully lifted the lid of each one. Then he shook his head in disappointment.

"Haven't you any jars with lids that don't make a noise?" he asked wistfully.

•

ANGRY SEVEN-YEAR-OLD: I'm leaving home. Call me a taxi.

•

"Dear Dad, guess what I need most? That's right. Send it along. Please. Soon. Best wishes. Your son, Russ."

"Dear Russ. Nothing ever happens here. We know you like your school. Write us another letter. Jim was asking about you at noon. Now we must say good-bye, Best wishes, Dad."

•

The happy new father bought his infant son a five-hundred-dollar bond. "With that," said the proud parent, beaming, "he'll be able to take his mother and me out to dinner the day he graduates from college."

During the weeks before Christmas eager Eddie was frequently told, "If you're not good, Santa Claus won't bring
you anything."

Eddie tried. He really did his best. But he didn't always
succeed, and he knew it.

Christmas morning finally came. Eddie had hardly slept
that night for worrying about some of his recent escapades.
He rushed downstairs, looked under the tree, seized the
biggest package, and unwrapped it. It was a marvelous
electric train.

He looked at it, rubbed his eyes and looked again, and
then said in an awed voice:

"Gosh! I couldn't have been *that* good!"

Uncle Ebenezer handed Hughie a five-dollar bill, saying, "Now be careful with that money, Hughie. There's a wise old saying, 'A fool and his money are soon parted.' "

"But I'd like to thank you for parting with it just the same, Uncle," said Hughie.

Donald had a hard time understanding why he should do something like homework when he didn't enjoy it. His mother tried to explain what duty was.

"Think of your father," she said. "He's a good example: he goes to work every day—not because he enjoys it, but because it's his duty. Can you imagine him doing something only because it's fun?"

"Oh, sure I can," said Donald.

"What?" she asked.

"Well, he married *you*, didn't he?" replied Donald with his most ingratiating smile.

Little Willy told the department-store Santa Claus what he wanted for Christmas, and emphasized that the most important item on his list was an electric train.

"But," said his mother, standing by, "you already have one, Willy."

"*That* one's Daddy's," said Willy. "I want one of my own."

•

RANDY: What's a grandparent?
SANDY: Oh, that's an old person who never had any children and doesn't know what to say to you.

•

While the new house was being built, the owner left notes every day for the workmen, politely calling their attention to mistakes or oversights.

Two weeks before he and his family were to move in, the floors still were not finished, the baths were not tiled, and the kitchen fixtures were not installed. On moving day, however, the house was in perfect condition. A few days earlier the owner had posted this message:

"After May 15, all work will be supervised by my four children."

•

The little girl at her first party refused a second helping of ice cream, though she eyed it longingly.

"Do have some more, dear," urged the hostess.

"Mother told me to say 'No, thank you,'" replied the little girl. "But," she added, "I don't think she knew how small the helpings were going to be!"

LOOPY LOUIS: My mother wants a dozen diapers for the baby.

SALESGIRL: That will be four dollars for the diapers and twenty cents for the tax.

LOOPY LOUIS: Don't bother about the tacks, miss. We use safety pins at our house.

•

YOUNG SCHOLAR: I learned to write in school today.

DELIGHTED MOTHER: What did you write?

YOUNG SCHOLAR: I don't know. I haven't learned to read yet.

•

Eight-year-old Debby came home from school and announced that she was going to marry Frankie.

"Does he have a job?" her father inquired, peering over his evening paper.

"Oh yes. He empties the teacher's trash basket!"

Legal Laughs

A boy was up before the court for automobile theft. When all the evidence had been heard, the judge asked the jury for a verdict of Not Guilty.

The jury retired for two minutes, and when they returned, the foreman rose and said, "Your Honor, we find the boy who stole that car Not Guilty!"

•

It was the end of a hot, sultry afternoon in the courthouse, where a slippery type named Sam was accused of stealing a bicycle. The evidence against him had seemed overwhelming, but his lawyer had managed after endless questioning to tie up the chief witness against him into a tangle of contradictions. Sam sat listening with open admiration.

Finally his lawyer called Sam to the stand and the judge, trying to put an end to it all, cut through the confusion of questions to say:

"Sam, answer me just one simple question: did you, or did you not, steal that bicycle?"

"Well, sir," said Sam, scratching his head, "I certainly *thought* I did, at the beginning. But this lawyer of mine has sure raised a doubt in my mind, and I'm not sure now whether I did or I didn't!"

A law professor was doing his best to instill a little knowledge of the subject into a collection of rather backward students.

One morning he gave them a long lecture on the whole question of making a will, and at the end of it he thought he would test their memories.

"Now, then," he said, "what are the essentials to a last will and testament?"

Nobody answered for a moment, and then a student at the back of the room spoke up.

"A dead person—and some money, sir," he hazarded.

The criminal lawyer to his secretary: "Take a threatening letter!"

•

A shoplifter was arrested for wearing an expensive pair of boots out of the store.

His defense: "I just happened to fall through the store window and these boots just seemed to become attached to me."

JUDGE: You are charged with having broken into the same shop on five occasions within a week, and yet you stole only one dress. How is that?

PRISONER: Well, yer see, yer Worship, I only pinched a dress fer me missus—but she made me change it four times.

•

It really happened, and got into the newspapers: there was a court hearing concerning a contested will and the judge asked one of the witnesses: "Do you have any brothers or sisters?"

"No, sir," replied the witness. "My only sister died 150 years ago."

The judge's mouth dropped open. "That's impossible," he stated.

"No, Your Honor. My father married at the age of twenty and had a daughter. She died in infancy. When my father was 72 he became a widower. He married again. Four years later I was born, and I am now ninety-four."

•

A municipal office employs "trusties" from the local state prison for some of the necessary duties around the place. For several years the janitor acted as a minister. He was well-shaven, performed his job well, and had earned his parole.

Before leaving he brought in his successor—a man convicted for embezzling a bank—whom he introduced as "one of my very best deacons."

He added proudly, "We're getting some very good men in the state prison these days!"

Two convicts were hauled into the warden's office for fighting during lunchtime.

The warden asked the cause of their quarrel and one of them said:

"He called me a dirty number!"

•

Harried Harry was found guilty of driving while under the influence of alcohol and the court ordered his license suspended.

"But I don't have a driver's license," confessed Harry, shamefacedly.

The judge deliberated and then issued a new order. Harry was to obtain a license, which would then be revoked.

MRS. GUSH: "Do you know that the police are looking for a man with one eye named Murphy?"

MRS. LUSH: "Do tell! And what is his other eye called?"

●

Goofy Gus was tried for theft and found Not Guilty.

He grinned. "Does that mean I can *keep* the money, Your Honor?" he asked.

●

Mr. Humbug was hurt in an automobile accident and sued for damages. The case dragged on, and months later a friend met him, still hobbling along on crutches.

"Do you still need those crutches?" his friend asked.

"I'm not sure," said Mr. Humbug. "My doctor says I don't, but my lawyer says I do!"

The judge in the small town surveyed the prisoner, who was accused of stealing an overcoat.

"I remember you, Shifty," said the judge, after a moment's reflection. "Three years ago you stood before this same bench on the same charge—stealing an overcoat."

"Well, yes, Your Honor," replied Shifty. "But how long can a secondhand overcoat last?"

•

Grandpa's hobby was changing his will. Every few months he called his lawyer in and dictated a new one, adding phrases that occurred to him.

This time he said, "Where it reads, in the beginning, that I'm of sound mind, I want to put: 'especially regarding foreign policy.' That will fix my son-in-law!"

•

A man was on trial for murder, and his prime defense was the fact that he had not been out of sight and sound of other people for more than two or three minutes.

In the course of his summing-up, the prosecuting attorney said to the jury:

"Ladies and gentlemen, I will hold my watch up in front of you. We will all wait, silently, for three minutes. This will give you an opportunity to judge what the defendant might have been capable of doing in that space of time."

The judge, the jury, the entire courtroom sat through what seemed an interminable length of time. Finally 180 seconds ticked away and the prosecutor announced that he had completed his case.

The jury was not out for long. It returned a verdict of Guilty.

JUDGE: I see you're accused of driving up a one-way street.
SUSPECT: I was only *going* one way, sir.
JUDGE: But didn't you see the arrows?
SUSPECT: Arrows? There weren't even any Indians in sight.
JUDGE: And where were you going?
SUSPECT: That's just it, sir: I must have been late, because everyone else seemed to be coming back!

•

A big-city real estate tycoon, wanting to raise rents in his most expensive apartment house, tried to evict a tenant illegally. The knowing tenant replied in writing—and it was one of the shortest notes ever penned. The exact words were:

"Sir, I remain. Yours truly."

The sheriff burst into the back room of the general store late one night and found four old cronies, apparently in the middle of a poker game—against the law in that town.

"Playing cards again, eh?" he shouted.

"Not me, sheriff," said the first. "I just dropped in to chat."

"Not me," said the second, "I'm just warming myself at the stove."

"As for me," said the third, "I came by to get a can of beans for my supper."

The sheriff turned on the fourth man, who was holding cards in his hand. "Now *you*," he said triumphantly, "you can't deny that *you're* playing cards!"

"Me?" The old fellow lifted his brows in astonishment. "But who would I be playing *with*?"

An Indian petitioned the judge for a new name.
"What is your name now?" asked the judge.
"Big Chief Screeching Train-Whistles," said the Indian.
"And to what do you wish to change it?"
"Toots," replied the Indian.

•

The sergeant to the suspect: "I assume the arresting officer gave you the usual warning?"

Muddled suspect: "Yes, sir. He said if I didn't come along quietly, he'd clobber me!"

The pretty witness was questioned by the judge about the shot that had been fired.

"Did you *see* the shot fired?" he asked.

"No, Your Honor, but I *heard* it."

"That is not sufficient," he ruled. "Step down, please."

As she left the box she looked at the jury and laughed. The judge fined her for contempt of court and admonished her severely.

The witness paused a moment, then asked, "Did you *see* me laugh, Your Honor?"

"No, but I heard you."

"That is not sufficient, Your Honor," she reminded him.

The fine was canceled.

●

The local precinct received a call from an almost incoherent householder, reporting that he had been struck down in the dark outside his back door by an unknown assailant.

A squad car was dispatched immediately and reported back soon afterward. "I solved the case," said the policemen, glumly.

"Very fast work," said the sergeant. "How did you do it?"

"*I* stepped on the rake, too," the cop said sadly, touching the growing lump on his head.

Medical Madness

PATIENT (on first visit to psychiatrist): The reason I need your advice is because I have developed the habit of making frequent long-distance telephone calls to myself.

PSYCHIATRIST: Making long-distance calls to yourself sounds like a rather expensive habit.

PATIENT: Oh, it doesn't cost me anything, I always reverse the charges.

A prim young man visited his doctor, who, discovering no obvious ailments, asked, "Do you smoke?"

"Never, it's a nasty habit."

"Do you drink?"

"Of course not! I disapprove of alcohol."

The doctor became more and more curious. "Have you ever kissed a girl?" he asked.

"I shall never kiss a girl until I am united in the bonds of holy matrimony!"

The doctor pondered. "Do you have pains in your head?"

"No, none at all."

"Strange, I thought your halo might be too tight. Tell me then, do you have pains in your back?"

"As a matter of fact, I do," said the young man.

"Aha!" exclaimed the doctor. "I knew that I was on the right track. You haven't learned to fold your wings properly in the subway!"

A psychiatrist interviewed a girl for a job as his secretary. He explained about the kind of patients who came to him for help.

"There's one," he said, "who thinks that little men follow him everywhere he goes. So last time he was in, I suggested that he open the door a little way, slip through quickly, and shut the door. Then the little men wouldn't have a chance to get in."

"And did they?" the girl asked breathlessly.

•

Doctors can be as absentminded as professors at times. There was one in Kansas City who came down to breakfast one morning, his head filled with all the calls he had to make before performing a difficult operation.

His wife came around and put her hands over his eyes, and when he opened them, there was a new set of golf clubs leaning against the table.

"For our wedding anniversary, darling," she said.

"Well, thanks," he said with some embarrassment. "And when it's yours I'll give *you* something nice, too."

The insomniac was delighted when his doctor gave him such an inexpensive prescription for getting to sleep.

"One apple before bedtime," said the doc.

"Wonderful!" The patient started to leave.

"Wait, that's not all," cautioned the doctor. "It must be eaten in a certain way."

The insomniac paused to listen to the rest of the prescription.

"Cut the apple in half," said the doctor. "Eat one half, then put on your coat and hat and go out and walk three miles. When you return home, eat the other half."

The patient had been seeing a headshrinker for some months because he thought he was a poodle. One day a friend asked him how the treatment was progressing.

"Well," said the patient, "I can't say that I'm cured yet, but I've made some progress. My psychiatrist has stopped me from chasing cars."

•

Sour Sarah said that she refused to take the tranquilizers her doctor prescribed because when she did she was nice to people she detested.

MR. OLDDER: Doctor, remember you told me last year to go out with women to get my mind off my business?

DOCTOR: Yes, how did it work?

MR. OLDDER: Fine. Now can you recommend something to get my mind back on business?

Mrs. Patter's maid took to her bed one afternoon, seeming really quite ill, and the family physician was telephoned to come quickly.

When Mrs. P. left him alone to examine the patient, the maid confessed: "Doctor, I'm not sick at all. I'm just pretending. That old tightwad owes me four months' back salary and I'm not getting out of this bed till she pays me!"

The doctor's face brightened. "She owes me for my past ten visits here," he declared. "Move over."

•

Burglars stole a 500-pound safe from a drugstore in Omaha, Nebraska. Inside the safe was $100 worth of ointment designed to soothe aching muscles.

There was a doctor who seemed to have a talent for attracting odd types. One day a farmer came in for a general checkup for life insurance.

"Have you ever had a serious accident?" asked the doctor.

"No."

"Ever had *any* accident?"

"No."

"I must say that's unusual. You mean to say you've never had a single accident in your life?"

"Can't say I have," replied the farmer. "Course, last spring when I was out in the west pasture, a bull tossed me over the fence."

"Don't you call *that* an accident?" the doctor probed.

"Absolutely not," said the farmer. "I know for a fact that durned bull did it on purpose!"

The doctor was explaining the new recovery techniques to his patient.

"You should begin walking as soon as possible after the operation. On the first day you must walk around for five minutes, the second day for ten minutes, and on the third day you must walk for a full hour. Do you understand?"

"Yes, Doctor," said the apprehensive patient. "But is it all right if I lie down during the operation?"

•

"It's obvious that the old miser isn't going to pay any attention to the bills I sent him," a dentist told his wife one day. "So I've decided to go up to his house and collect in person."

An hour later he was back, looking very dejected. "I can see by your face that he didn't pay you," said his wife.

"He not only didn't *pay* me," said the dentist ruefully, "but he bit me with my own teeth!"

•

"Joan," said the young man, inching closer on the sofa, "I've been thinking how wonderful it would be if you'd marry me. Have you any objections?"

"Dough," she replied at once.

He rose, picked up his coat, and headed for the door. "I might have known you'd think of that first," he muttered bitterly.

He banged the door and headed out into the night, heartbroken.

She collapsed in tears, also heartbroken. "I *said* dough, I had dough objections. Whaddever went wrog?" she sobbed through the cold in her nose.

DOPEY DAN: Why did the house call for a doctor?
DIZZY LIZ: Because it had windowpanes.

•

The little girl of a famous doctor always introduced herself as "Dr. Patterson's daughter." Her mother said one day, "That sounds so pretentious, Dotty, Just say that you're Dorothy Patterson."

Not long afterward one of her father's friends met her on the street and said, "Aren't you Dr. Patterson's little girl?"

"I used to think so," said Dotty doubtfully, "but my mother says I'm not!"

PATIENT: Doctor, a terrible thing has happened. I've lost my memory!
DOCTOR: How long has this been going on?
PATIENT: How long has *what* been going on?

A world-famous woman pianist had to enter a hospital, and the admitting clerk asked her occupation. "Pianist," she said.

"Housewife," murmured the clerk.

"Pianist—or musician," insisted the artist.

"I'll just write housewife," the clerk persisted.

And then the next question was: "What is your husband's occupation?"

"Just write housewife," snapped the irritated pianist.

•

A psychiatrist and a friend were walking down the street, and a stranger passing by suddenly kicked the psychiatrist in the shins. The headshrinker walked on as if nothing had happened.

His friend was astounded. "Aren't you going to do anything about it, Doc?"

"No," said the psychiatrist. "That's *his* problem."

•

The little girl asked the druggist for some castor oil that couldn't be tasted. He said he'd look up some suggestions in his book and meantime offered her a lemonade.

When she had drained the glass he said, "Well, did you taste it?"

She gasped. "You mean the castor oil was in the lemonade? But it was meant for my mother!"

Neurotic Nonsense

During a time of distressing drought an anxious amateur agriculturist went to a shop and bought a barometer. The salesclerk was making a few explanations about indications and pressures when the customer interrupted impatiently, saying:

"Yes, yes, *that's* all right—but what I want to know is how you set the thing when you want it to rain?"

•

A meek little man came in to the county seat and explained his problem to the health officer.

"We all live in a one-room cabin out there on the mountain," he said. "Myself and my six brothers. One of them keeps three greyhounds, another has a mountain goat with a weak chest that mustn't go out, Mike has his wolfhound in the cabin, and Spike has his five budgies. Francis keeps two parrakeets. The air is terrible and the smell is shocking."

The health officer was sympathetic, but he saw a solution.

"Surely you could open a window to let in some fresh air."

"Open the window! What about my fifteen pigeons?"

"Ladies and gentlemen," shouted the street performer, "in a few moments I will astonish you by eating coal, stones, and nails, and I will also swallow a sword, after which I will come around with the hat, trusting to get enough for a crust of bread."

"What!" came a voice from the crowd. "Still hungry?"

•

On a holiday visit to his uncle's farm, a little boy from the city came upon a farm worker dealing with a slaughtered pig.

"What are you doing to it?" asked the boy.

"Getting it ready to be cured," he was told.

The boy gazed intently as the animal for a moment, then declared:

"You're a bit late, it looks awful dead to me."

At the new movie, the couple occupying the seats in front were a man and his dog. When the picture was over, the dog applauded enthusiastically.

The man behind leaned forward and said, "That's simply astonishing!"

"Yes it is," said the dog's companion, "especially since he hated the book."

•

Thoughtful Theodore muses: It isn't a swelled head that hurts, it's the shrinking that has to be done.

•

A harried priest, looking at the clock: "Could you possibly come back tomorrow for confession, Reilly, my lad? You haven't committed a murder today, have you?"

"Indeed I haven't, Father." On his way out he met O'Rourke. "Don't bother going in tonight, Paddy, Father's only hearing murderers tonight."

•

"I wish to make a complaint," said a man to the Post Office official. "For some time I have been receiving some most impertinent and threatening letters. How can I stop them?"

"I think we can help you," replied the official. "Have you any idea as to where these letters come from?"

"Oh yes. From the Income Tax people."

•

Loopy Louis surprised his girl friend with a new fur coat. She'd never seen him in one before.

A world-famous scientist was watching the heavens through the huge telescope at a large observatory. Suddenly he announced, "It's going to rain."

"What makes you think so?" asked his companion.

"Because," said the astronomer, still peering through the telescope, "my corns hurt."

"My wife thinks she's a chicken," the husband explained to the psychiatrist.

"That's a serious delusion," was the reply. "How long has this been going on?"

"Three years."

"Why didn't you bring her in before now?"

"Well," replied the embarrassed husband, "we needed the eggs."

MR. FUSSBUDGET: Sir, your son has been walking on my brand-new cement sidewalk before it had dried!
NEIGHBOR: Well, I can't scold him for that. Boys will be boys, you know. Don't you like kids?
MR. FUSSBUDGET: Oh, indeed I do, but in the abstract, not in the concrete.

•

Mrs. Fuddledy kept going back to her dentist to have her false teeth ground down because they didn't fit.
"Well, this is the last time I'll do it," he said, "because I can see that they fit your mouth perfectly."
"Did I say anything about my mouth?" she asked petulantly. "They don't fit in the glass at night."

•

The farm lad looked up at the man who offered him a ride, then looked carefully at the pony and trap. Without a word he climbed into the trap and remained standing, the sack of potatoes still upon his back.
"Put the sack on the floor and sit down," suggested the man. The boy shook his head.
"That poor old pony got enough to do pulling us two, without this sack of 'taters!"

•

DINER (in roadside cafe): Two eggs, please. Don't fry them a second after the white is cooked. Don't turn them over. Not too much grease. Just a small pinch of salt on each. No pepper. . . . Well, what are you waiting for?
WAITER: The hen's name is Betty, and she's a Rhode Island Red. Is that all right, sir?

The doctor said consolingly, "Young man, within six weeks of amputating your legs I'll have you on your feet again."

•

SMART ALECK: I know a guy who calls his girl friend Candy Bar.
SOBER SAM: Why? Is she that sweet?
SMART ALECK: Nope. Because she's half nuts.

•

"Is your little boy insecure, Mrs. Muffins?"
"Well, I don't know about *him*, but everybody else in the family certainly is since he arrived."

•

Dopey Dan was puzzled by the headline in the newspaper:
"LOCAL MAN TAKES TOP HONORS IN DOG SHOW."

Clever Chris says that the difference between a psychotic and a neurotic is that the psychotic thinks that two and two make five. The neurotic knows that two and two make four—and he *hates* it!

•

A restaurant sign: "Eat here and you'll never live to regret it!"

•

A man excitedly ran up to another man on the street and slapped him heartily on the back.

"Paul Porter," he greeted him. "Am I glad to see *you*! But tell me, Paul, what in the world happened to you? Last time I saw you, you were short and fat; all of a sudden you seem tall and thin."

"Look, sir," the puzzled man answered, *"I'm* not Paul Porter."

"Ah!" boomed the undaunted greeter contemptuously. "Changed your name, too, eh?"

•

The great psychiatrist was examining the patient.

"What would happen if I cut off your left ear?" he asked.

"I couldn't hear," the lad replied.

"Then what would happen if I cut off your right ear?"

"I couldn't see," the boy said.

The great psychiatrist became alarmed. "This is serious. Why do you say you couldn't see if I cut off your right ear?"

"Because my hat would slide over my eyes!"

The store manager heard a clerk say to a customer: "No, madam, we haven't had any for a long time."

"Oh yes, we have," interrupted the manager. "I'll send to the warehouse immediately and have some brought over for you."

The customer burst into hysterical laughter and walked out of the store. The manager turned to the clerk. "Never refuse anything!" he said furiously. "Always send out for it. . . . What did the lady want?"

"She had just remarked," explained the amused clerk, "that we hadn't had any rain lately."

•

PSYCHIATRIST: Mrs. Nutts, you have acute paranoia.
MRS. NUTTS: I came here to be examined, not admired!

•

Worried Wilfred couldn't sleep one night for wondering about the headline in the paper that day:

MAN REFUSED TO GIVE UP BITING DOG.

You see, Wilfred just loves dogs.

•

A psychiatrist once said that cows are very bitter and neurotic because, like taxpayers, they get tired of being milked.

•

DOPEY: A shepherd sold a third of his flock for a hundred dollars. What would the rest of the flock realize?
NOTSO DOPEY: It would realize that some of the sheep were missing.

Harried Harry was sure that he'd swallowed a horse, and no one could convince him that it was his imagination. Finally his friends took him to a psychiatrist, who put him to sleep and brought a big white gelding to the bedside.

"There you are, Harry," said the doctor. "I've removed the horse from you."

But Harry just shook his head miserably. "You're trying to fool me. You see, *my* horse is a black mare."

•

A famous actor was asked how he had achieved such a long life.

"I believe," he said, "that it is due to the fact that I never smoked, drank, or looked at a girl—until I was ten years of age."

•

INQUISITIVE IKE: I see you're putting up a new building.
WORKMAN: Yup. That's the only kind we ever put up.

•

Sign on apartment: SAXOPHONE FOR SALE.
Sign on neighboring apartment: HOORAY!

'Orrible Outrages

The three ladies met for their usual Wednesday lunch and, as usual, split responsibilities.

Plump Polly said, "Today, Rena, you keep track of the money, Blanche will do the ordering, and I'll count the calories."

•

Mrs. Golfwidow was so annoyed at being left alone every weekend that she took up bowling one Sunday.

"Well, how did it go?" her husband inquired amiably that evening.

"Well, at least I didn't lose any balls!" she said triumphantly.

•

The most poorly paid clerk in the company managed to support a wife and four children and to own a beautiful house, an expensive car, and a weekend cottage in the country.

"How in heaven's name do you manage?" asked his boss. "You only make $110 a week!"

"Well, you see, sir, there are 863 people working in the plant, and every week I raffle off my wages for $1 a chance."

An English couple showed their American guests around their country cottage.

"You know," said the host proudly, "this is the oldest house in the country!"

"Well, don't worry about that," consoled one of the Americans. "It's a lovely place even so—and it's yours."

•

A $10,000 limousine shot past an old wreck of a car on a country road. The driver leaned out and hollered:

"Hey, what's making that awful racket in that contraption of yours?"

"I reckon," answered the country guy, "it must be the $9,500 jingling in my pocket."

QUERULOUS HOUSEWIFE: I want to make a complaint about those bananas I bought from you yesterday. They were green and awfully hard to peel.

GROCER: And what do you expect at that price, madam? Zippers?

•

The executive came to his first consultation with the psychiatrist saying that in the last few weeks he hadn't slept or eaten a decent meal, and had lost twenty pounds.

"Do you have any idea what causes this anxiety?" asked the headshrinker.

"I know exactly what causes it," said the executive. "My wife and I went for a month's tour of Europe, and when I came back I found that my business was in better shape than it has been in ten years."

•

A famous naturalist had many visitors to his botanical gardens, examining the unusual results he achieved from crossbreeding.

He was usually the politest of men, but one day a woman stayed too long, asked too many silly questions, and sorely tried his patience.

Her final question was: "Are you working on some new plant right now?"

"Why yes," he said. "I'm trying to cross eggplant with milkweed."

"How fascinating!" she exclaimed. "And what will be the result?"

"That should be obvious, madam," he replied. "Custard pie."

DONNY: The walls in our place are so thin we can hear the neighbors changing their minds!

RONNIE: That's nothing, ours are so thin that we can not only hear their radio, we can see their television!

•

A meticulously groomed lady entered a store and purchased two packages of invisible hairpins. As she paid for them, she asked, "Are you absolutely *certain* these hairpins are invisible?"

"Lady, I'll tell you how invisible they are," the clerk assured her. "I've sold three dollars' worth of those pins this morning, and we've been out of them for two weeks!"

•

In the old country, marriages weren't made in heaven, but by marriage brokers. These experienced gentlemen interviewed applicants carefully so that they could make successful matches.

There was one who was a bit hard of hearing and relied on his daughter during an interview. His first question was always, "How old are you?"

One applicant replied, "I'm young. In the early twenties."

"What did she say?" he asked his daughter.

"She said she was young in the early twenties," his daughter dutifully reported.

•

Modern life is noisier than we realize. One evening a harassed mother sat up in alarm and cried:

"What just stopped?"

Alfie bought a very loud new sports jacket and the next day was hunting about among his shirts and ties for the right thing to go with it. He asked his wife's advice.

"Well, I'll tell you something that *won't* go with that jacket," she retorted. "That's *me!*"

•

The customer ordered filet of sole and waited with keen anticipation. After the dish was served—and it was a very watery one—he waited some more.

WAITER: Is anything wrong, sir?

CUSTOMER: Not really. I'm just waiting for the tide to go out a bit.

•

CUSTOMER: How much are the cigars?

COUNTERGIRL: Two for a quarter!

CUSTOMER: I'll take one.

GIRL: That'll be fifteen cents.

SECOND CUSTOMER (overhearing transaction): Here's a dime. Give me the other one.

•

A group of parents were discussing what measures they would take if they woke up to discover a burglar in the house.

One said that he kept a shotgun handy. Another thought tear gas would be a good idea. The third opted for a good alarm system connected with the local police station. The fourth, father of five small children, said wearily:

"If a burglar came into my room at night, I'd get up and take him to the bathroom."

Two country club matrons were asking the club's professional about golf lessons.

"Do both of you ladies want lessons?" asked the professional.

"Oh, no, thank you," said one, "*I* learned last week."

Obnoxious Oliver kept making demands of the waiter in a loud voice that disturbed the other restaurant patrons. At one point he shouted:

"What do you have to do to get a glass of water around this joint?"

"Why don't you try," asked the man at the next table, "setting yourself on fire?"

•

The boss showed the new girl around the plant and proudly pointed out the computer.

"It's replaced twenty-seven men," he said.

"This isn't the job for me," she commented, heading for the door.

BROKE: How do you spend your income?
BUSTED: About 30 percent for rent, 30 percent for clothing, 40 percent for food, and 20 percent for amusement.
BROKE: But that adds up to 120 percent.
BUSTED: Don't I *know* it!

•

Shouldering his way through the Christmas crowds, Father reached the sports department and purchased a motorcycle for his son.

"What a surprise your boy will have," said the kindly saleslady as she made out the charge slip.

"Indeed he will," replied the father. "He's expecting a Ferrari."

•

GOOFY GUY: Do you know what an astronaut sandwich is made of?
CLEVER CLAUDE: Sure. Launch meat.

Plane Problems

Bettina and her grandmother were making a flight together. Suddenly Grandma heard the stewardess address another passenger by a well-known name, and she rushed over to get his autograph, having a few words with him while she hovered over his seat.

Very impressed, Bettina asked her how she'd managed to get the famous autograph. "Oh, I just told him how much we enjoyed driving our Chrysler."

Bettina said nothing. For the name on the slip of paper was Fritz Kreisler.

•

Nervous Nellie canceled her trip at the last minute when she heard the announcement:

"Flight 408 to Albany is now ready for its final departure."

•

The new automatic plane was making its first cross-country flight. A recorded announcement said:

"This is the first all-electric jet. There is no pilot, no crew. Press a button and we take off. Press another button and dinner is served. Press another button and we land. Nothing can go wrong, can go wrong, can go wrong, can . . ."

A young cowboy rushed into a bank in a small California desert town and cried:

"Cash this quick, please, will you? I've double-parked my helicopter."

And so he had! It was in the middle of the bank's parking lot, tied down next to a horse and buggy.

•

The night operator at the airport kept getting irate calls from a woman living nearby complaining about the noise of the engines. The operator kept explaining that it was due to the wind direction, and that there was nothing he could do about it.

"Then let me talk to someone who *can* change it," she demanded.

He referred her to another telephone number, and never heard from her again. The number was that of "Dial-a-Prayer."

On the next trip the tired businessman tried a new gambit to still a talkative seatmate. When his companion opened by asking, "Going far?" he replied:

"Only as far as Chicago. I am a stockbroker, aged fifty-two, my wife's name is Helen, I have two sons in college, I own a house in Connecticut, two cars, a cocker spaniel, and a $20,000 mortgage. Anything else?"

•

An elderly man, on his first plane trip, was disturbed as he peered out the window and saw the wing-tip light blinking and blinking.

Finally he hailed a stewardess and said timidly, "I wonder if you'd mind telling the pilot that he's left his turn indicator on?"

•

PHIL: What makes you so sure that flying's safe?
BILL: If it wasn't, would they be letting you fly now, pay later?

•

From a small-town newspaper: The door prize at the Elks Club Dinner—a two-weeks trip to Nassau—was won by a man who had left the day before for Nassau.

•

Out in the Golden West where gallantry still exists, a woman struggled with a flat tire on the desert highway while cars whizzed by without stopping.

But suddenly a light plane landed alongside, the pilot quickly changed the tire, and then he took off again.

It was a hot summer night, and the drive-in movie was filled to capacity. The movie was a thriller about fighter planes.

At the climax, the hero was bringing his plane in for a difficult landing and the airport lights were on the blink. The man in the control tower in the movie shouted through the loudspeaker system:

"Everyone in cars, turn on your lights!"

Instantly, every car in the drive-in switched on full headlights.

•

A tired businessman on a plane trip, wearied with making conversation with his youthful seatmate, suggested a game of riddles.

"If it's a riddle you can't guess, you give me $5 and vice versa."

"Fine," said the student. He thought a moment and then said, "But since you're so much older and wiser, I'll give *you* only $2.50."

The businessman agreed to this and said, "You go first."

"What bird has four legs swimming and two legs flying?"

"I give up," said the businessman. "Here's $5.00. What's the answer?"

"I don't know either. Here's $2.50."

•

KATE (at the airport): I wish we'd brought the television set with us.

NATE: What on earth for?

KATE: Because I left the plane tickets on top of it!

128 •

Every year the clerk's heart fell as Mrs. Muchmoney approached his counter on her way to her winter home in Florida, because every year the same scene took place.

The lady traveled with heaps of excess luggage and it was his job to weigh it all and tell her the price of the overweight—this year, an even $90.

The usual ranting and raving followed, and the poor clerk stood there silently taking the abuse. Finally Mrs. Muchmoney, deciding that she'd just about run out of scathing things to say, wound up by announcing:

"And what's more, I'll never use this airline again!"

The young clerk shook his head. "Promises, promises," he muttered.

•

Dopey and Loopy were going to make a flight together and couldn't decide who to name as the beneficiaries of their plane insurance. They settled it by naming each other and boarded happily, arm in arm.

•

A gentleman in his seventies got his nerve together and took a flight in an airplane. As he climbed out after the ride, he turned to the pilot and said:

"Sir, I wish to thank you for both of those rides."

"What are you talking about?" said the pilot. "You had only one ride."

"No, sir," said the passenger, "I had two: my first and my last!"

Queer Quandaries

It was a very suspenseful moment in the middle of an exciting murder picture; an elderly gentleman began groping and reaching around for something on the floor, thereby greatly disturbing the lady in the next seat.

"What have you lost?" she finally snapped at him.

"A gumdrop," said the man unhappily.

"You mean to say that you're going to all this trouble—and bothering everyone around you—for a measly little gumdrop?"

"Yes," the man replied. "You see, my teeth are in it."

•

MAN ON AFRICAN SAFARI: Is that elephant safe?

WHITE HUNTER: Much safer than *we* are!

•

The violinist apologized for his performance by saying that he'd had to play by ear.

"Painful, wasn't it?" remarked his friend. "That's the way we had to listen."

•

ROB: What have a crab, a woman, and a diplomat in common?

BOB: You never know whether they're coming or going.

The shopper spent some time trying on and thinking about the coat, trying it on again—and then finally deciding against buying it.

"It looks too much like what my friends think I can afford," she explained to the somewhat bewildered saleslady.

•

A fisherman was having a wonderful time in a trout stream. The fishing season hadn't opened and he had no license. After a while a stranger walked up.

"Any luck?" asked the stranger.

"Any luck! Wow!—this is a great spot! I took thirty-eight out of this stream yesterday."

"By the way, do you know who I am?"

"No."

"Well, meet the game warden," said the stranger.

"Oh." The fisherman paled, then made a comeback. "Well, do you know who *I* am?"

"No."

"Well, meet the biggest liar in the country."

A very great pianist, new to New York City, was immediately so popular among the city's leading social lights that he scarcely found time to practice. In desperation, he instructed his butler to tell all callers, regardless of their importance, that he was not at home.

One morning, Countess X—the top social hostess of them all—telephoned, just as the pianist was practicing one of his most difficult pieces.

"The master is not in," said the butler dutifully.

"I can hear him playing," snapped the great lady.

"Oh, no, madam," the butler assured her. "That's just me, dusting the keys."

•

CHRIS: If you have six haystacks in one corner, two in another, three in another, and nine in the middle, and put them all together, how many would you have?

CARL: One.

•

At a party a white-haired lady somehow found herself barricaded in a corner by four young men. For almost an hour they talked—about baseball, the stock market, the latest records, fishing, the best way to make a martini—just about everything. The lady found it impossible to edge her way out and stood there, lighting her own cigarette, a captive listener.

Suddenly one man became aware of her presence and said, "Gosh, I'm so sorry! You must have been very bored with all this talk."

"Oh, no," she said. "I've always wondered what young men talked about when they were alone."

A famous after-dinner speaker was invited to appear at a club in a medium-sized city. As he stepped up to the lectern after the dessert had been served, he noticed that the usual pitcher of water and glass were missing. He called the chairman's attention to the oversight.

"Do you want the pitcher of water to drink?" asked the chairman.

"No," replied the speaker sarcastically. "I finish with a high-diving act."

A rather youthful, much too plump, modern granny went on a diet, and the next time she came to visit, her little grandson exclaimed with great concern:

"But, Grandma, where did you leave the rest of you?"

The absentminded professor was walking across the campus when a student stopped him and asked for a dollar. The professor gave him one but later complained to a colleague:

"The boys in this college are always asking me for some money."

"But *that* one was your *son!*" exclaimed his friend.

•

PARKER: My wife says that if I don't give up drinking, she'll leave me.

BARKER: That's too bad, old chum.

PARKER: Yes, I suppose I'll miss her.

•

One rainy day—no taxis to be had—a very famous female news-broadcaster squeezed into a crowded city bus, fearful of being late for her broadcast.

She stood there, panting from her rush for the bus, and a courteous gentleman started to rise, but the lady pushed him back into his seat.

"Oh, no—don't get up for *me*," she said. "None of this old, worn-out false gallantry. I'm a healthy working woman and I can stand just as well as the next one."

On his fourth attempt, the gentleman thrust out his jaw and said firmly, "This time you simply *must* let me get out, madam. I'm eight blocks past my stop now!"

•

Highway sign near a small New England town:

"This may be the jet age, but don't pretend you're flying one through here."

Toscanini had a painful experience one evening with a soloist who began his cadenza bravely enough but soon got into difficulty. Obviously flustered, he wandered farther and farther off-key. The maestro and the entire orchestra held their breaths. Just before their cue to resume playing, the soloist managed to recover the original key. Toscanini bowed and said, "Welcome home, Mr. Ginsberg."

●

Thoughtful Theodore thinks that only a mediocre person is always at his best.

●

LANDLADY: Since you didn't eat anything, I won't charge you for your breakfast.
VISITOR: Wonderful! . . . I didn't sleep all night, either.

Ridiculous Road Tales

Wise Wilfred always says that you should drive in such a way that your license expires before *you* do!

•

It is the custom in some small garages to identify cars by the names of their owners. This leads to some interesting entries in the work book.

Mrs. Jones won't start.

Give Miss Prim some alcohol. Two quarts should get her going.

Wash Professor Higginbottom.

•

HANK: I have an annoying noise in the back of my car.
FRANK: Make her sit in the front seat.

•

Mrs. Chitter took her brand-new Volkswagen out for a spin and, to her horror, it stopped dead in the busiest part of town and wouldn't start up again. She opened the hood and, with astonishment, discovered that she had no engine!

At that moment, Mrs. Chatter drew up alongside in a similar car and said soothingly:

"Don't worry, dear. It so happens that I have a spare engine in the rear and I'd love to lend it to you!"

A young man from Mississippi was driving in New York City and found himself in a dispute with a pretty girl when both of them were trying to get into the same parking place. He had seen it first and knew that he had a right to it.

Furious, she rolled down her window and cried, "I thought you Southerners were supposed to be so polite!"

"Oh, we are, ma'am," said the young man, grinning. "And any time you're in Mississippi I want you to be *my* guest!"

A minister was hurrying to the sickbed of a parishioner and was surprised when a traffic policeman approaching him motioned to him to pull over.

He knew that he'd been speeding, and meekly accepted the ticket the policeman made out. But, he asked, how had the officer been able to know that he was speeding, when he was coming from the opposite direction?

The cop pointed solemnly to the sky and said, "Someone up there told me!"

Respectfully, the minister raised his eyes toward heaven —and saw a traffic-spotter helicopter circling overhead.

Hubby reluctantly agreed to give his wife driving lessons. After some months she had learned how to start and stop the car and was pretty good at changing gears. However, she still had difficulty with traffic rules.

One day she stopped for a red light, and stayed, and stayed, and stayed. Finally her husband sighed and pointed out the traffic cop, who was frantically motioning her to get going.

"Go!" said the exasperated husband. "Or are you waiting for *him* to turn green?"

•

PARKER: Know how to learn to think fast on your feet?
BARKER: How?
PARKER: Cross the street against the lights.

The pretty girl failed her driving test for the third time and burst into tears. "I'm so nervous in traffic!" she explained to the inspector.

"Well, miss," he said sympathetically, "why not try again in three months?"

"But I *have* to drive—back and forth from the airport. You see, I'm a pilot!"

•

Luscious Lucy was working in her front garden one day in a rather brief bathing suit when a patrol car stopped. The officer got out and introduced himself.

"Would you mind telling me how long you've been working here in the yard, miss?" he asked.

"About an hour."

"That's what I thought." He nodded. "You see, we had a very successful radar speed trap set up just down the road. About an hour ago traffic slowed up considerably. In fact, miss, if you keep on working in your garden like this, you'll put us out of business!"

•

MA (warningly): That woman driving in front has her hand out, Pa.

PA: The only thing *that* proves is that her window's open.

•

Clever Chris says that the livestock in his part of the country must be expected to have a sense of responsibility, because on a recent drive in the country he saw this sign:

HORSES, PLEASE KEEP THIS GATE SHUT.

The Fussbudgets had some weekend houseguests who were taking a long time about leaving. Finally the explanation was forthcoming.

"The statistics say that this holiday weekend there will be thirty deaths in traffic accidents," explained one of their visitors. "And we're waiting until the quota has been met."

•

Coming home one evening with a crumpled fender, Dizzy Liz explained to her husband:

"I was doing just what you always tell me to do, dear. I was looking out for the unexpected."

"So?" he intoned angrily.

"Well," she replied meekly, "I *hit* the unexpected."

A philosopher, after his wife smashed up his new sports car, remarked calmly:

"Well, that's the way the Mercedes Benz."

Vague Vera was flagged down by a traffic cop who accused her of wandering over the double line three times, ignoring a stop sign, and making an illegal U-turn.

She was furious. "Why," she asked him, "do you spend time plaguing respectable citizens when you should be on the lookout for drunken drivers?"

"Madam," he replied, "that's just what I thought I had caught *this* time!"

•

The driver of the bakery delivery truck told the policeman that the reason he was speeding was so that the whipped cream on the cupcakes wouldn't turn sour!

•

A Quaker, backing his car, bumped into the one behind him. The driver jumped out and called him several very insulting names.

When he ran out of names the Quaker said gently, "If you offer a man something and he refuses it, to whom does it belong?"

The other driver was taken off-balance. The he replied: "To the one who originally offered it, I suppose."

The Quaker smiled. "Good!" he said. "I refuse the abuse and ugly names you have offered me."

•

Gloomy Gus comments that nowadays "when you go out for a ride on a Sunday, you have to spend all your time figuring out the road signs, and you don't get any time to look at the scenery. . . . Fifty years ago people would have just left the directions up to the horse."

PROFESSOR: I say there, you in the automobile! Your tubular air container has lost its circularity.

MOTORIST: What?

PROFESSOR: The cylindrical apparatus that supports your vehicle is no longer symmetrical.

MOTORIST: Huh?

.PROFESSOR: The fabric surrounding the circular frame whose revolutions bear you onward in space has not retained its pristine rotundity.

MOTORIST: Are you nuts?

PROFESSOR'S WIFE: He means you have a flat tire.

•

Two middle-aged ladies backed and filled repeatedly until their car was cozily ensconced in a no-parking zone. The traffic cop who had been watching the whole operation strode over and asked very politely:

"Would you two ladies like a ticket?"

They looked at each other inquiringly and then the one in the passenger seat shook her head and explained gently, "I'm so sorry, young man—it's nice of you, but you see we never win anything."

•

Mrs. Gadabout thought her husband was just too cautious a driver. They were always late for engagements because he drove so slowly. But nothing could change his ways.

"I'd rather be patient for five minutes," he explained, "than a patient for five months."

142 •

Scholastic Shilly-shallies

A famous novelist was asked by a student how he got ideas for his books.

"Well," he said, "imagine me coming down in the morning, sitting at the breakfast table, and starting to eat my eggs and bacon. I have just taken a delicious mouthful when my wife says, 'Richard, the mechanic says the car can't be fixed and we need a new one.' Right then and there I get the idea for another novel."

•

TOMMY: My teacher says I have to write more clearly.
MOTHER: That's a very good suggestion. You should.
TOMMY: But then she'll know that I can't spell!

•

On a jet flight to Rome a famous novelist found himself seated next to a four-star general.

"My son wants to go to West Point," said the novelist. "He gets straight A's in school and he has invented a marvelous device for monitoring radio broadcasts on the other side of the world."

Much impressed, the general pulled out pencil and paper and asked, "What's his name and his age?"

"His name is Jonathan," replied the novelist, "and he's seven years old."

A co-ed emerged from English II in despair.

"What's the trouble," asked her roommate, "Chaucer or Shakespeare?"

"Neither," sighed the co-ed. "It's the spelling on my themes. The professor told me that whenever I'm in doubt I should consult a dictionary."

"Well, that's simple enough," her roommate consoled her.

"But I'm never in doubt!" moaned the co-ed.

•

The prisoner dug for months, and when he had completed his tunnel he found that he had come up in a school playground. As he emerged into the open air he shouted exuberantly at the nearest little girl:

"I'm free!"

"That's nothing," she said scornfully.

"*I'm* four."

"What is the meaning of the word *average*?" asked the teacher.

"Hens use it to lay eggs," replied the top boy in the class.

"What do you mean, Bobby?" the puzzled teacher asked.

"Well, I read the other day that hens lay one egg each day on an average," Bobby explained patiently.

The Dean of Women at a well-known university was surprised when a young male student walked into her office one day and said he needed her advice on some matters.

"You're in the wrong office, aren't you?" she asked.

"No, ma'am," he said. "I represent most of the men on campus and we decided you were the one to come to for advice because most of our problems are—women!"

•

TEACHER: This is the fifth day you've had to stay after school, Mike. What do you think of that?
MIKE: I'm sure glad it's Friday!

Some children were invited to participate in the ground-breaking for a new Sunday school building. Each child very solemnly turned over a small shovelful of dirt.

Afterward the grandfather of one little girl asked what had happened at church that morning.

"Well," she replied dejectedly, "we dug for a new Sunday school, but we didn't find it."

•

SECOND-GRADER: Did your watch stop when it hit the floor?
FIRST-GRADER: Of course! You didn't think it would go *through*, did you?

•

The teacher came home from the first day of school and sank wearily into a chair.

"I gave my seventh grade students an aptitude test today," she said to her sympathetic husband, "and found that every one of them is best suited for the sixth grade!"

•

Lazy Larry read in the local newspaper that there was a crowded school situation in his community. The next day he went to the principal's office and offered to help alleviate the problem: he would remove himself from the school.

•

A bandleader asked his pianist to give piano lessons to his young son. At the first lesson the pianist said to the boy, "Do you know the scale?"

"Yes, sir," the nine-year-old answered without a moment's hesitation. "One hundred bucks for sidemen, and double for the leader."

The child came home in floods of tears from Sunday school. When her parents were able to quiet her a bit, they asked what had happened.

"The teacher said that God loves us all," she whimpered.

"But of course He does," her father said comfortingly. "Why should that make you cry?"

"He doesn't love *me*," she sniffled.

"What makes you think that?" her mother asked in amazement.

"Because I tried it on a daisy . . . and it came out . . . it came out . . . He loves me not!"

•

HORACE: I forgot my gloves!
MORRIS: Why didn't you tie a string around your finger?
HORACE: Gloves are warmer than strings, dope!

•

A third-grade Pennsylvania boy was asked to write a short description of Quakers. He chewed on his pencil for a while and then put down:

"Quakers are very meek, quiet people who never fight or answer back. My father is a Quaker, but my mother is Irish."

•

TEACHER: What is seven times five, George?
George hung his head and said nothing.
TEACHER: Now, George, suppose I have five fives and you have two fives and we put them together. Who do we have?
GEORGE: Canasta!

The teacher wanted to know how the physical features of our country had influenced its history. The whole class thought for a while, and then Precocious Perry raised his hand:

"If it hadn't been for the Delaware River," he said, "Washington couldn't have crossed it!"

•

A graduate student working on juvenile delinquency reported in a New York University sociology seminar that he was having difficulty in collecting data. His project was to telephone a dozen homes around nine in the evening and ask the parents if they knew where their children were at this hour.

"My first five calls," he lamented, "were answered by children who had no idea where their parents were!"

The young farm wife took her eldest to school to register him. One of the questions on the form she was given asked:

"Language spoken in the home?"

She paused for a moment and then wrote in:

"Nice."

•

TEACHER: If I cut a steak into four parts, what do I have?

CLASS: Quarters.

TEACHER: What will I have if I cut those pieces in half again?

CLASS: Eighths.

TEACHER: Again?

CLASS: Sixteenths.

TEACHER: Suppose I cut the pieces again. What will I have?

VOICE (from back of room): Hash!

•

Little Paul was given a bowl of alphabet soup for dinner. He put down his spoon in disgust.

"It's Saturday!" he protested. "Can't you even let a guy forget school on *weekends*?"

•

The teacher had been trying to interest her class in the intriguing problem of Noah's hobby during the time of the Flood.

"I think," she said, "that Noah must have spent his time fishing."

"Miss," broke in a young lad, "he couldn't have caught much with only two worms."

• 149

TEACHER: Do you know what a hypocrite is?

JOHNNY: A hypocrite is a boy who comes to school smiling.

•

A kindergarten tot was assigned to make a Christmas drawing of the stable where Christ was born. She worked all afternoon on it and showed it to her father when he came home from work.

He studied it carefully and then pointed to an item that puzzled him and asked what it was.

"Oh, that?" the child exclaimed. "That's their television set."

•

Motherly Molly told the teacher, "Before I got married I had six theories about bringing up children. Now I have six children and no theories."

Terrible Truths

Two mind readers were having dinner together. There was silence for several minutes, then one of them looked up expectantly.

The other snorted, "That joke is old as the hills! But have you heard the one about . . ." and they roared with laughter.

•

A rookie policeman stopped a driver for speeding. But the driver said, "I'm a sergeant on the traffic detail, off-duty at the moment."

The rookie glanced at the police sergeant's credentials—and went right on writing out the ticket.

"Now look here," blustered the sergeant, "someday you might be sent to the traffic detail. Just remember, I'll be your boss there!"

The rookie smiled and handed over the ticket.

"I hope, sir, that when I get there you'll remember that you have a good man working for you!"

•

LODGER: What's the weather like today?
LANDLADY: Rather like your bill.
LODGER: How do you mean?
LANDLADY: Unsettled.

The members of the congregation were rather surprised to read in their church bulletin one morning:

"Subject, Sunday: 'Is there a Hell?' A warm welcome awaits you."

•

The beggar walked down the street and asked a man for twenty cents for a cup of coffee.

"But a cup of coffee costs only ten cents," objected the gentleman.

"I know," said the beggar, "but I wanted to invite you to join me!"

•

DUPE: Why is the sea so restless?
DOPE: Because it has rocks in its bed.

Mrs. Hobson sought out the headwaiter at a grand dinner-dance and asked him, "What's become of that pretty waitress who was taking the cocktails around?"

"I'm sorry, madam," apologized the headwaiter, "could I get you a drink?"

"No," said Mrs. Hobson, "I want to know what happened to my husband."

•

A young merchant marine officer was making his first trip as third mate, and after a few turns at the wheel on the high seas, under the watchful eye of the captain, he was beginning to feel confident in his ability to run the great ship.

However, as they neared their first port of call, he learned that *he* was to be on watch, and that *he* was to guide the vessel down a narrow channel and to a neat berthing.

He brooded about this for a while and then that morning at breakfast he said, "Captain?"

"Yes?"

"We've got wheels under this ship, haven't we?"

"Wheels?" The captain stared, his bacon halfway to his mouth.

"Yes, sir. I'd like to feel that wherever I steer this boat today—it'll go!"

•

BAFFLED SALESMAN: A low handicap?

DAFFY DORA: Oh, I *do* hope you know what one is, because my husband has always wanted one and I want to surprise him for his birthday!

A visitor exclaimed over the painting of Verbena Abernathy, the Grandma Moses of the Ozarks.

"What an incredible talent," she exclaimed. "Oh, how I wish I could take those glorious colors home with me!"

"Don't worry, you will," cackled Verbena happily, "you're sitting on my palette."

PLUMBER (having fixed leaky faucet): That will be ten dollars, please.

HOUSEWIFE: Ten dollars for five minutes' work!

PLUMBER: Sorry, we have to charge the hourly charge—ten dollars on each service call. It's the boss's orders.

HOUSEWIFE: Well then, sit down and talk to me for fifty-five minutes. I've paid for it, and I'd like some company while I have my coffee.

The young couple were trying to make their fortune running a small motel and diner on a mountain road. Business wasn't very good, so one evening they were delighted when a family of six walked in—parents and four small children.

The mother took the children into the rest room and the father ordered a cup of coffee. A few minutes later the mother emerged with the four tots all scrubbed and in their pajamas, ready to bed down outside in their station wagon.

All the comforts of a motel for the price of a cup of coffee!

•

HE: Do you think I'm bigheaded?
SHE: No, why?
HE: People as handsome and charming as I am usually are.

•

Two children carefully dialed long distance to sing "Happy Birthday" to their grandfather. As soon as the phone was picked up they piped out the tune in very bad harmony, only to be told, "Sorry kids, but you have the wrong number.

"But don't worry," the strange voice went on, "you needed a rehearsal. Now dial again!"

•

Someone asked Romantic Rena why she didn't get married again.

"I have a dog that snores, a parrot that swears, and a cat that stays out all night," she told them. "What could I possibly want with a husband?"

The little boy scout came home sobbing. His mother gathered him up and asked him anxiously what was wrong.

"They've expelled me from the troop," he sobbed.

"Why on earth did they do that?"

"I was helping a little old lady across the street and she got run over!"

•

One minister said to another, "We know what the world will come to in the end, but what on earth's going to happen in the meantime!"

IRK: What did the ship weigh before it left port?
JERK: I don't know, what?
IRK: Anchor.

•

Lazy Larry's definition of a business conference is that it's a way to get other people to share your troubles.

•

The mother of a large brood went every day to a psychiatrist.

"There's nothing wrong with me," she explained to her neighbors, "but that's the only place I can lie down for an hour's nap without being disturbed."

•

The boarding house was patronized by a sporting crowd. One evening the landlady put a platter of *very* thinly sliced meat on the table. One sport turned to the other and said:

"You cut, I'll deal!"

•

COUNTRY BOB: That farmer's a cruel man.
COUNTRY SLOB: What makes you say that?
COUNTRY BOB: See how he's pulling the ears of corn!

•

WIFE: Darling, my doctor told me today that I needed a change in climate.
HUSBAND: Lucky you, dear. The TV weatherman just now predicted a change for tomorrow!

"Where have you been for the past three hours?" asked the pastor's wife.

"Well, I met Mrs. Jones on the street and asked her how she was feeling," sighed the exhausted parson.

Useless Undertakings

A famous mind reader stopped a little boy on the street and said, "Say, Cyrus, can you tell me where the post office is?"

"How did you know my name is Cyrus?" asked the child in amazement.

"I'm a mind reader, son. I was right, wasn't I?"

"Yeah, you sure were. So you must know where the post office is." And he turned away.

•

The absentminded professor was very excited one day while he was spading up his garden to discover an assortment of coins—pennies, nickels, dimes, and quarters.

"Eureka!" he cried. "I've discovered buried treasure!"

"And I," said his wife, "have discovered another hole in your pocket!"

•

An elderly professor was thought by many to be a bit odd. His neighbor was certain of it the day she saw him holding a sprinkling can over a window box.

She called out to him, "Professor, there's no bottom in that sprinkling can."

"That's all right," he replied gently. "These are artificial flowers."

Hopeful Harry bought a paint outfit and read the directions inside:

"Take the palette from the box, squeeze some paint onto it from the tubes, dip your brush in the paint, and daub the canvas with it. Rembrandt, Michelangelo, and all the other great painters used this very same method."

•

The private asked the lieutenant if they shouldn't warn the general not to smoke near the munitions dump, as it might blow up.

"Don't be silly," said the lieutenant. "It wouldn't dare!"

SANDY: How come the foreman fired you, Andy?

ANDY: Well, you know what a foreman is—someone who stands around and watches other men work.

SANDY: What's that got to do with your being fired?

ANDY: Well, he just got jealous of me, I guess. People kept thinking *I* was the foreman.

•

MRS. NAGS (watching her husband trying to sew on a button): You've got the thimble on the wrong finger.

MR. NAGS: I know. It should be on yours.

•

A famous artist with a great sense of his own importance painted the portrait of the governor of his state.

"But," protested the governor, "it doesn't *look* like me."

"Then try to look like your portrait," replied the artist. "*It* looks very good indeed."

•

CUSTOMER: Half a dozen oysters, please—not too big, not too small, not too cold, and not too warm.

WAITER: Certainly, sir. And how large a pearl would you like?

•

Mike was always known as a good mimic, but when he burst into song one evening and did a marvelous version of a Puccini aria, his friends were astounded. "I had no idea you sang so well," one of them said.

"Oh, I don't sing at all," said Mike. "I was just imitating Caruso."

STAGE MANAGER (to matronly woman at stage door): So you wish to see Ming Soo Ling, the great Chinese Wrestler?

MATRONLY WOMAN: Yes, tell him his mother is here from Ireland.

•

When a man came home by taxi late one night and climbed out of the cab, he realized he'd dropped his wallet inside. He stuck his head inside the window and said:

"Would you mind turning on the overhead light? I've dropped my wallet, and as it has several hundred dollars in it . . ."

He pulled his head out just in time as the cab jerked forward and raced out of sight at fifty miles an hour.

•

"Did you hear about the singer who wore his hair over his eyes so he could start the show off with a bang?"

•

The boys in the class were so noisy that the teacher told them they must all add and write down all the numbers from 1 to 100. The boys groaned and settled down to a long morning's labor.

All but Brilliant Billy. He thought for a moment, then wrote a number on a piece of paper and handed it to the teacher. She was stunned. It was right!

"How on earth did you do that, Billy?" she asked.

"Well," he said, "100 plus 1 is 101; 99 plus 2 is 101, and so on down to 51 plus 50 is 101. I have 101 50 times, which is 5050."

Three men were sitting on a park bench. The one in the middle was sleeping, the other two were going through the motions of fishing.

They would cast, reel in, and pretend to examine their catch, and toss it into a bag.

After watching this for some time a policeman strolled over, shook the man in the middle awake, and asked,

"Are these two nuts friends of yours?"

"Yes, they are," he said.

"Well, then, get them out of here."

"Sure thing," the man replied, and began rowing vigorously.

A famous pianist was giving a concert in a small hall. In the middle of a piece a phone started ringing loudly just off stage, and his audience was in a torment of embarrassment. Without missing a note the pianist said:

"If that's for me, tell them I'm busy for the next eight minutes."

A suburban housewife finished balancing her check-book and adding up the month's bills, then made a big decision.

She went next door and knocked on the door and said, "Mabel, I want to make a deal with you: *I'll* stop keeping up with *you* if *you* stop keeping up with *me*."

Vacation Vagaries

There was a bachelor man-about-town who was fortunate enough to be able to retire in the prime of life and who headed for the south of France expecting to find ideal weather in midwinter.

To his dismay it was often chilly, often windy, and frequently drenched with rain.

He went to the American Express office at Nice and asked, "Where, in the entire world, can I swim in January?"

The clerk thumbed through various reference books and announced that it would be quite safe to go to Ecuador and, in fact, that there was a small freighter leaving for that South American country in four days' time.

"Fine!" said our man-about-town. "But wait a minute —how many passengers does it carry?"

"Twelve, sir," replied the clerk.

"Twelve. Hum! But suppose there are none among the other eleven who can do the samba!"

•

An American who'd just made a tour of Europe dropped into his local barbershop and bragged that a haircut in Switzerland cost only sixty-five cents.

"Yeah," the barber sympathized, snipping away. "But think of the fare!"

On a torrid July day in New York, Mrs. Moneybags boarded the ocean liner for England, headed straight to her first-class cabin, unpacked her luggage, then headed in high dudgeon for the purser's office.

"Young man," she thundered. "My cabin is like an inferno! I have never been so uncomfortable in my life. Are these the conditions offered on a British ship?"

"I'm frightfully sorry, madam," the purser replied. "But you must realize this is *your* weather, not *ours*."

•

A self-made millionaire was making his first trip around the world in a chartered plane, and on a very limited schedule, between business deals, the pilot tried to make the trip instructive.

"That's Athens down there," he said at one point.

"Never mind the details," snapped the millionaire. "Just mention the continents!"

•

In these days when you can have breakfast in New York and dinner in Rome, it's difficult to imagine the days of the old whaling ships when it was commonplace for a voyage to last up to ten years. Once, in those days, the mate of a ship about to leave port came up to the captain and said:

"Sir, your wife is out there on the dock, crying her eyes out."

"What on earth for?"

"She says you didn't kiss her good-bye."

"But, good grief, man," said the captain, "I'm only going to be gone for two years!"

166 •

On the ship en route to a job assignment in France, a young executive was given a flash course in the language.

He had been in Paris for only two days when a big limousine pulled over to the curb and one of the passengers inquired, in French, which way it was to the railway station.

The young executive was delighted to find that not only could he understand every word they said, but he could give them the right directions. Laboriously, he told them which turns to take; they thanked him politely and, as they drove off, he heard one say to the other in perfect New Yorkese:

"Now that is the first French I have been able to understand at all!"

•

A seaside hotel had a guest book and each departing client was asked to write his name, and add a comment if he wished.

The proprietor was proud of his book, but was always puzzled by the remark written after one name:

"Quoth the Raven—"

•

A couple at the resort hotel were constantly complaining about the weather. It was either too hot or too cold, too cloudy, or too windy, or too wet.

The weary hotelkeeper kept politely agreeing and then one day said in sympathetic tones, "At least you're better off than *I* am, sir."

"And how is that?" asked the tourist.

"*You* can go home," replied his host.

An infuriated guest at a small-town motel grabbed the phone and growled into it, "Are you the desk clerk of this dilapidated joint?"

The nettled clerk replied, "Yes I am. What's eating you?"

"That," said the guest coldly, "is what I'd like to know."

A tourist driving from Paris to Nice stopped to pick up a young man running pell-mell down the road.

"You must be in a great hurry," remarked the driver as the youth climbed into the front seat.

"Not really," replied his passenger. "I always run like that when I want a ride. It never fails!"

•

Flying Fanny complains that it would have made much more sense if only the early settlers had built their cities nearer the airports.

The lady next door did the Grand Tour of Europe and returned home in rhapsodies about the architecture, and with several pounds of slides which, unfortunately, she hadn't taken the trouble to label.

A much-traveled professor came to call one evening and said, "Wasn't the Parthenon a sight to remember?"

"My dear!" exclaimed the traveler, "Rome was enchanting!"

"And the Colosseum?" he asked wryly.

"Ah—Geneva!" she exclaimed, her hand over her heart. "When I think of the Christians and the lions I could weep!"

A diner in a New York restaurant looked on anxiously as a stranger took the diner's topcoat off the hook and put it on.

"I beg your pardon," he said at last, "but are you Bertram Rogers?"

"I am not," said the stranger, reaching for a hat.

"Well, that's Bertram Rogers' coat you've just put on," said the timid diner.

"And who, may I ask, is Bertram Rogers?" asked the stranger, disappearing through the door.

A guest at an elegant Miami hotel glared disapprovingly at his daughter's new bikini, and remarked:

"Anne, it's just big enough to prevent your being tanned where you ought to be!"

A nature-loving couple drove through New England at the height of autumn. They filled the back seat with autumn leaves on whole tree branches, as well as wild flowers and rhododendron bushes.

As twilight fell they lost their way and stopped to inquire of a farmer.

"Should we take this road back to Boston?" they asked him.

"Might as well," he said, surveying the car. "Looks like you've taken everything else we've got up here."

A visiting Englishman was taken to the top of the Empire State Building, the highest man-made creation on earth.

His host pointed out the sights—New York harbor aswarm with ships, New Jersey on the right, Brooklyn on the left—and, below, the island called Manhattan, set like a jewel in a circlet of rainbow waters.

The people on the streets seemed like ants, the buses like slightly larger insects.

"Well?" his host asked eagerly, expecting a stunned response.

"Hum," intoned the Englishman. "Gives one rather an impression of height, doesn't it?"

•

TAXI DRIVER: Hey, buddy, I forgot to throw the meter and I don't know what to charge you.
VISITING SCOTSMAN: Oh, that's all right. I've forgotten to bring any money and couldn't pay you anyway.

•

The two men met as they were taking the footpath leading to lookout point—one going up, the other down.

"How are you, O'Leary?" asked the climber.

"Not bad at all, O'Reilly, but my name isn't O'Leary."

"Well, mine isn't O'Reilly—so it can't be either of us!"

They nodded amicably and each proceeded on his way.

Wartime Weirdies

The jet pilot was a marvelous fighter and had quite a few medals to prove it. But he was thoroughly disliked by everyone who knew him. When his commanding officer finally contrived a way to transfer him to another unit, he recorded on his papers:

"Excellent officer at 7000 feet. Should never be permitted to come any closer to the ground."

•

A wealthy young draftee appeared at his first formation wearing handmade English shoes.

The sergeant paused, looked down at the well-shod feet in disbelief, and then inquired sarcastically, "May I ask what you're wearing those things for?"

"They're mine, sir."

"Oh, so they're yours, are they? And would you wear a top hat and tails if you had them here?"

"Not with brown shoes, sir!" exclaimed the draftee, in horror.

•

The draft board received a politely worded letter that said in part:

"I spent four years in the last war, and I don't want to push in ahead of someone else who wants an unforgettable experience."

SERGEANT: Do you know that gun is loaded?
PRIVATE: It's all right, sir, I've got my finger over the hole.

•

Two lions escaped from the zoo. One headed into the city to see the bright lights; the other went in the opposite direction to enjoy the beauties of nature.

Several days later they met. The one who'd gone to the country was sleek and fat; the one who'd headed for the city was worn and starving. "I'm feeling awful," he said. "I haven't eaten more than a few scraps since we ran away."

The fat one sympathized. "Come on with me," he said. "I'm hiding in an army camp and I eat a second lieutenant every day."

"Gee! Aren't they out gunning for you?"

"Nope. They never even miss them."

The sergeant told the new recruit, "You're going on night patrol next week. I hope you're prepared for it."

"Oh, don't worry, Sergeant," said the recruit. "My mother is going to make the rounds with me until I get used to it."

Corrigan had served in the Irish Navy and after a while, wanting to see something of the world, he joined the American fleet. Quickly he became sad, and by the time they reached Japan he seemed on the verge of melancholia.

The captain sent for him. "Corrigan," he said, "you have the best conditions possible, and you're seeing the world—so what can we do to cheer you up?"

"Please, sir, could you let me cycle home to Dublin on weekends?"

•

The general was annoyed when the young sentry held him up to ask for the password.

"Don't bother with this idiot," he said to his driver. "Drive on."

"B-b-b-but before you go," said the agitated sentry, "just tell me whether I should kill you or the driver."

A young GI sat solemnly in his dugout, watching the artillery pounding an enemy post on a nearby hill, the ground shaking violently with each explosion.

Just then, a war correspondent seeking a Christmas-at-the-front story approached the GI and asked cheerfully, "Tell me, was Santa Claus good to you this year?"

"Good to me?" said the GI miserably. "Twenty years ago I asked Santa Claus for a soldier-suit—and now I get one!"

•

The new GI complained about sand in his stew.

"You came here to serve your country," said the tough sergeant, "not to complain about the food!"

"Yessir, but I came here to *serve* my country, not to *eat* it."

The colonel's wife made the most of her position at the army base and usually carried on long monologues about her husband's achievements and medals.

One day she turned to the young bride of a second lieutenant and said patronizingly, "My husband is a colonel, and yours . . .?"

The bride grinned. "My husband is twenty," she said, "and yours . . .?"

•

A nurse in an army hospital was writing a letter for a soldier whose hand had been wounded. He began by dictating, "The nurses here are all very ugly. . . ."

"Now look here!" cried the nurse. "I don't think that's a bit nice!"

The soldier grinned. "No, it's *not* nice, nurse—but you can't imagine how happy my wife will be when she reads it."

•

The army psychiatrist asked the inductee, "Do you ever go out with girls?"

"No," said the boy.

"And why not?"

"Because my wife won't let me."

•

PADDY: I've picked the girl, but I haven't asked her yet.
LADDY: And what if she refuses you?
PADDY: Then she's as stupid as all the other women are.
LADDY: If they're all stupid, why do you want to marry one?
PADDY: And what else *is* there to marry?

178 •

The French girl asked the American soldier what "GI" meant.

"Girl Inspector," he said gravely.

•

The Navy chaplain asked some recruits what they wanted most out of their Navy service.

The first said: "To serve my country."

The second said: "To see the world."

The third said: "What do I want most out of the Navy? Me!"

•

SERGEANT: Hey, you can't go in there. That's the major's tent.

GREENHORN: Then what have they got "Private" over the door for?

A soldier was filling out a questionnaire and paused at the question "How long has your present employer been in business?"

After a moment he wrote: "Since 1776."

Xuberant Xotica

One of India's richest maharajas engaged a crack American engineer to construct a dam. The job, completed in record time, was perfect, and the delighted maharaja, besides paying the substantial fee agreed upon, tried to present the engineer with a basketful of gleaming rubies. The engineer would have none of them, however.

"I'm pleased you like the job I did," he said simply, "but I can't take your rubies. We don't do things that way in America. The fee I set was more than adequate." But still the maharaja insisted.

"Okay," agreed the engineer, "but let's make it a token gift. Golf is my favorite recreation. If you gave me a couple of good golf clubs, we'd all be happy."

The maharaja agreed to this, and the engineer returned to America. Some three months later he received a cable from the maharaja:

"My agents have combed the United States," it read, "and selected three golf clubs, which I have bought for you. I am sorry to say, however, that only two of them have swimming pools."

•

DUPE: How do you make a cigar lighter?
DOPE: Take out the tobacco.

Fancy Fred sat down for lunch one day in the Savoy Grill and ordered Dover sole. When the waiter asked if Fred would like to have it boned for him, he said he'd do it himself.

Well, he'd just got his knife and fork poised, ready to start deboning, when the sole opened its left eye and looked at him in a pitiful way indeed, saying, to Fred's immense astonishment, "Please don't eat me!"

Well, poor Fred, that shook him! He got right up and left the restaurant, and he couldn't face the thought of eating Dover sole from that day on.

Then one of his friends told him that he shouldn't let such a thing get on top of him. "It's just like falling off a horse. Get back on again," the friend insisted.

So the next time Fred found himself in a restaurant, he ordered Dover sole. Then just as he was ready to debone the fish, it opened its left eye, looked at him, and said, "What's the matter? Can't you afford the Savoy Grill anymore?"

An out-of-work ventriloquist had no money left and was wandering down the street wondering what to do when a sparrow came and perched on his shoulder and to his surprise stayed there for several blocks. He decided to take a chance and use his talent in order to get a meal.

Walking into a restaurant, he ordered a steak dinner, then turned and asked the sparrow what he'd have.

"A rasher of bacon, underdone," replied the bird.

The waiter's eyes bulged. When he came back with the steak and the bacon, he brought the manager with him to watch them dine. The sparrow pecked at the bacon.

"Not bad," he commented. "We ought to come here more often."

This was too much for the manager. He wanted to buy the bird. But the ventriloquist refused. "We're old pals, you know."

But the manager finally persuaded him to take $100 for the sparrow. But as the ventriloquist started out the door, the sparrow looked up at him and said, "A fine pal you are! Selling me for a measly hundred bucks. Just for that I'll never say another word as long as I live!"

And he didn't.

•

The little boy wanted a bucket of salt water to take home with him and asked the lifeguard if he could have one. The lifeguard jokingly charged him ten cents.

The next morning the little boy came back to the beach when it was low tide. He gazed about for a moment and then said admiringly to the lifeguard:

"Gosh, you must have done a lot of business last night!"

It was closing time at Joe's Bar and the same four drunks were sprawled along the bar. Joe gathered them up and roughly deposited them in a taxicab.

"Here's ten bucks," he said. "Drop the guy on the left off at 245 Park Avenue, the one next to him at 24 East 57th Street, the third one at 1112 Park Avenue, and the fourth goes all the way up to Butler Hall in Columbia University."

The taxi drove off, but was back inside of fifteen minutes.

"Hey, Joe," cried the driver. "Will you please come over and sort these guys out for me again? I hit a bump on Fifth Avenue."

The kids were told to give father gifts that would interest him. One year they gave him a book called *How to Be a Successful Executive*. The next year they chose a book entitled *How to Improve Your Executive Ability*. The third year the volume was called *Don't Give Up the Ship*. And finally, they found *How to Cheat in Business*.

At the height of a top-level international conference an English magnate let out a cry of disgust. His valuable timepiece had been hooked. The chairman—prime minister of a great European power—was properly outraged.

"Gentlemen," he announced icily, "this is disgraceful. The lights will be extinguished for five minutes. All of us will leave this chamber in darkness. The thief, as he exits, will place the watch on the table there beside the door, where the buhl clock is standing."

The delegates filed out in silence. Five minutes later the room was relighted. Not only was the watch still missing; the buhl clock had also disappeared.

•

A missionary was captured by a band of cannibals. "Going to eat me, I suppose," he said. "You wouldn't like it."

And so saying, he took out his pocketknife, sliced a piece from the calf of his leg, and handed it to the chief. "Try it and see for yourself," he urged.

The cannibal took one bite, grunted, and spat.

The missionary remained on the island fifty years. He had a cork leg.

•

A teenager had just gotten her driver's license and was a little uncertain as she drove about town on her own.

At a main intersection she signaled the traffic policeman that she was going to make a left turn—and then remembered that the shop she wanted to go to was farther on.

She inched the car over to him and said, "I've decided to go straight, officer."

"Good for you!" he congratulated her.

The very exclusive cooperative apartment required business references, bank references, personal references, and church references.

Mr. Moneybags was able to supply the first three easily, but the only church with which he had any connection was the one where he'd been christened, and which his mother still attended. He wrote her, asking her to procure a letter from the minister. The letter arrived in due course:

"The subject was, according to our records, christened and confirmed in this church. However, we have no knowledge of him during the last twenty-five years."

•

The retiring secretary of the treasury graciously greeted his successor at the door to his office. With a sweeping gesture he made the new secretary welcome with the words:

"Nothing in the till!"

•

Mother went to the rummage sale and bought her son the jackknife he'd been wanting. Standing alongside her was a poorly dressed woman who wanted a baseball bat that was on sale, but who lacked twenty-five cents of the price. Mother gave her the twenty-five cents and forgot about the incident.

Several months later the woman stopped her on the street.

"You're the nice lady who gave me twenty-five cents to buy that baseball bat. I don't know how you've been doing with that jackknife, but my husband's been as good as gold ever since I've had that bat!"

186 •

PRIEST: Do you entertain evil thoughts?
MIKE: No indeed, Father, they entertain me.

•

The sultan fell in love at first sight with the visiting American's daughter.

"If you'll let me marry her," said the sultan, "I'll give you her weight in rubies."

"Give me a few days," answered the American.

"To think it over?"

"No, to fatten her up."

•

Roland's wife went off to spend two weeks with her parents and she was worried about how he'd get along without her. She phoned one evening and, anxious to reassure her, he said:

"There's nothing to worry about, darling. One of the girls from the office is here helping me with the housework!"

Youthful Yarns

PROUD NEW MOTHER: Last night the baby cried for half an hour without once stopping to take a breath!
BORED NEIGHBOR: What's the matter with him? Hasn't he any endurance?

•

A farmer's son came home from technical college and said his class was trying to find a universal solvent.

"What's that?" asked his father.

"It's a liquid that will dissolve anything," explained the boy.

"Great idea," nodded the farmer. "But when you find it, *what you gonna keep it in?*"

•

FEEBLE FLORA: Can you write in the dark, daddy?
FATHER: Of course. What do you want me to write?
FLORA: Your name on my report card.

•

Timmy kept running in for another apple. When he came in the sixth time within a couple of hours, his exasperated mother said:

"For heaven's sake, Timmy, no more. The way you go on you'd think they grew on trees!"

PROUD FATHER: My son's been walking since he was eight months old!

BORED CO-WORKER: Doesn't he ever get tired?

•

Mrs. Gadabout took Junior along on a shopping expedition, but it wasn't a success. When she stopped to look at something he pulled at her to get moving, and when she wanted to hurry along he lagged behind to look at something *he* was interested in.

Finally she said, "Junior, if you don't stop this behavior I'm going to spank you, right here on the street."

Junior looked around with interest. "Where will you sit?" he asked.

Randy went over to play at his friend's house but he came back a few minutes later. His mother asked him why.

"Well, something told me that his mother didn't want me there," he said.

"Did she say so?"

"No," Randy admitted. "But she led me out the front door and locked it."

Doubtful Dan went up to the minister after church. "I just can't see how God can answer prayers," he said.

"How is that?" asked the minister.

"Well, the man who sells coal was praying for cold weather, and the man who sells fruit was praying for warm weather, and the farmer was praying for rain, and the carpenter was praying for a dry spell. So how could God answer all their prayers?"

"Well," said the minister, "what's the weather right now?"

"Cold and rainy," said Dan.

"And what was it yesterday and the day before?"

"Mild and dry," said Dan.

"See?" said the minister. "Everyone gets what he needs, sooner or later."

●

The youngster whose only ambition in life was to be an astronaut was taken on a tour of Washington. His uncle pointed out the Washington Monument, and the kid's considered judgment was:

"They'll never get that thing off the ground!"

●

The librarian of a roving bookmobile was confronted recently by a worried-looking youth who demanded, "Where's that book you talked me into borrowing three weeks ago?"

The gratified librarian asked, "Did you like it so much you want to read it over again?"

"Gosh, no," said the young man. "I wrote my new girl's phone number in it!"

EXASPERATED MOTHER: How can you get into so much mischief in one day?

JACKIE: Well, I get up earlier than most kids.

IRK: If the king of Ruzzia was a Czar and his wife was a Czarina, what were their children?

JERK: Czardines.

There was a blizzard raging and Hopeful Harry ate his breakfast in front of the television set. His mother finally gathered his coat and boots and mittens and dumped them in front of him and said:

"Here, put them on. You've listened to three channels and if school was going to be closed you'd have heard by now."

●

LITTLE LILLY: Gertrude hit me!
MOTHER: I'll speak to her tomorrow, dear.
LILLY: You mustn't do that! Tomorrow's her party.

●

BOBBY: I'm feeding the monkeys half my peanuts.
ROBBY: That's nice of you.
BOBBY: Yes, I'm giving them the shells.

●

The phone rang and Cyrus ran to answer it. He came right back and said, "Daddy, Mack Murphy's father wants to copy my homework when you've finished with it!"

●

GROCER: Take a handful of candy, Johnnie.
JOHNNY: No, thank you.
GROCER (laughing): Don't be shy. Here.
And he put a handful in a paper bag and handed it over.
Outside, Johnny's mother asked him why on earth he hadn't helped himself.
"Because his hand is bigger than mine," said crafty Johnny.

VOICE ON THE PHONE: Is this the Salvation Army?
ANSWER: Yes, it is.
VOICE: Is it true that you save young girls?
ANSWER: Yes, it is.
VOICE: Well, please save me one for Friday night.

•

An English professor asked his class, "What did Shakespeare do in his experimental period?"—expecting the students to think about some of the earlier works of the Bard.

A hand shot up instantly and a sweet female voice piped up, "He married Anne Hathaway."

•

HORACE: I found fifty cents on the sidewalk.
MORRIS: That's mine. I dropped a half-dollar right there this morning."
HORACE: But what I found was two quarters.
MORRIS: That's it! I heard it break in two when it hit the pavement."

•

A majority of the members of the school board voted against spending money for new textbooks and the teachers struggled helplessly along with some that had been written decades before.

One evening the math teacher asked for an opportunity to speak to the board. He said, "I would like to read you the problem that I gave my class today."

It began, "If a plumber makes two dollars a day . . ."

"Stop!" cried the chairman of the board. That evening they voted unanimously for new texts.

Grandma was putting Smart Suzy to bed while her parents were entertaining guests downstairs.

"Those must be important people down there," Suzy said drowsily.

"What makes you think that?" asked Granny.

"Because Mommy's laughing at all Daddy's jokes."

•

TIM: I see you're working in your garden.
TOM: Yup.
TIM: What are you growing?
TOM: Tired!

•

The new neighbors had a big, exuberant collie who rushed up to Frankie and began licking his face affectionately. Frankie screamed.

The neighbor rushed up and asked, "Did he bite you?"

"No," whimpered Frankie, "but he tasted me!"

Zestful Zoology

The farmer came back from the county fair with souvenirs, a cow, and a rabbit, and then went quickly about the chores he had to finish by sundown.

When he came back into the farmhouse he discovered that his wife was stewing the rabbit for dinner.

"Good grief, woman!" he cried in dismay. "That rabbit could speak five languages!"

"Then why didn't it say something when I told the children we were having it for dinner?" she asked, logically.

•

RONNIE: Which ones are the ducks?

JOHNNIE: The ones that look as if they've been riding a horse all day.

•

A man and his wife were off for a spin in the country one lovely Sunday afternoon when suddenly a dog pulled up alongside, forced them to the side of the road, and whipped out a notebook.

WIFE: Whatever is that dog doing?

HUSBAND: Writing out a ticket, silly. Can't you see that it's a police dog?

Said the bluejay perched on the telephone wire to the other bluejay perched on the telephone wire:

"Did you ever notice the way some people's voices make your toes twitch?"

•

Timid Tillie woke in the middle of the night and heard a noise downstairs. Cautiously, she crept down and followed it to its source, in the kitchen. There she found her husband, Wilfred. Said Wilfred:

"I tried counting sheep and remembered the leg of lamb."

•

A big black horse trotted into a booking office one day and asked for a job. He said that he was a terrific magician and a better escape artist than Houdini.

The booking agent was astonished as the horse did a series of fancy card shuffles, a slick rope routine, and pulled a dozen chickens out of a plaster egg.

"Say!" said the agent. "That's pretty good. But tell me, can you do any disappearances?"

The horse gave a disgusted snort.

"Don't be ridiculous," he said. "Whoever heard of a horse that could disappear?"

•

The thoughts of a rabbit on sex
Are practically never complex.
A rabbit in need
Is a rabbit indeed;
And his actions are what one expects!

Man's best friend is often written up in the classified pages of the newspaper. For instance:

Collie, one-year-old, for sale, will work sheep or cattle, hunt any distance, and stop to whistle.

* * *

Wanted, a new pair of football boots, for a good young cocker spaniel.

•

Leo the Lion was feeling his oats one fine spring morning and went out to the watering hole looking for trouble.

The first to arrive was a gorilla. Leo grabbed him, pinned him down, and asked, "Who is king of the jungle?"

"You, O wonderful creature," gasped the gorilla.

Leo purred with satisfaction and next pounced on a tiger.

"Who's the boss around here?" asked Leo in threatening tones.

"But you, who else?" replied the tiger plaintively.

The third to arrive for a drink at the watering hole was an elephant. "And who," roared Leo, "is the master of all Africa?"

The elephant grabbed Leo with his trunk and bashed him against a large boulder. Leo got up, shook himself, and said reproachfully to the elephant:

"Just because you don't know the answer you don't have to get rough!"

•

"Waiter, there's a fly in my soup!"

"Don't worry, sir, the spider on the bread will take care of it."

Silas Scrooge was bitten by a mad dog, but the doctor came quickly.

"Doctor," he said, "give me a sheet of paper and a pen."

"You're all right, Silas," said the doctor. "You don't need to make out your will."

"Will, indeed!" snarled Scrooge. "What I want is to make out a list of people I'm going to bite!"

•

DOPE: Did you hear about the rooster who stayed up all night to see where the sun went?

DUPE: Nope.

DOPE: Finally, it dawned on him.

•

The weekend fisherman was approached by the warden, late on the Saturday afternoon.

"Sorry, sir, but you can't fish without a permit," said the warden.

"Oh, that's quite all right," replied the fisherman. "I'm doing very well with worms, thank you!"

•

The professor of logic contrived an ingenious question for his class. He asked it the minute the students entered Monday morning:

"What would you think if you saw nine elephants walking along the road with red socks on, and one elephant walking along behind with green socks?"

His brightest student put up his hand.

"That nine out of ten elephants wear red socks, sir," he responded.

They have a way of weighing hogs in Texas; they get a long plank, put it over a crossbar, and tie the hog on one end. Then they find a stone that will balance the weight of the hog on the other end. And then they guess the weight of the stone.

•

Father welcomed his son back from his fishing vacation. "Did you use flies?" the father asked.

"You bet we did, Dad. We fished, cooked, ate, and slept with flies!"

•

LITTLE LOUIE: Mama, the zoo was wonderful! There were lions and lionesses, tigers and tigresses, elephants and elephantesses, and bears!

•

They were shooting a film in the African wilds. Said the director to the star:

"Now, you run two hundred yards beyond the canyon and then stop. The lion will be fifty yards behind you. Get it?"

"Yeah," said the star. "But does the lion?"

•

JUDY: What's long, black, and thin, and says "Hith, Hith!"?
JODY: A snake with a lisp.

•

THOUGHTFUL THEODORE: When it comes to common scents, my money's on the skunk.

After each drink at the local pub Murphy took a frog from his pocket, put it on the counter, and stared at it. Finally the barman could no longer contain his curiosity and asked Murphy what he was up to.

"Well, you see, it's this way," said Murphy, "so long as I can see one frog it's all right. But when I see two of them I have to do something."

"And what is it that you do?" asked the barman.

"I pick up the two of them, put them in my pocket, and go home," said Murphy.

•

The symphony conductor was rehearsing the second movement of the Beethoven Ninth when the violinist's cat meowed. The maestro slammed down his baton and shouted, "Someone take that cat out and have it tuned properly!"

HELEN HOKE's first job was with her father's county newspaper, which he owned and operated in a small town in Pennsylvania, U.S.A. Since then she has been a primary school and university teacher, bookshop manager, and Director of the Children's Book Departments of several publishing houses in New York, including that of Franklin Watts, Inc.

Author and editor of many children's and adult books, Helen Hoke has been for over fifteen years Director of the International Projects Division of Franklin Watts, Inc. She is married to publisher Franklin Watts, and lives in London, England.